PRENATAL TESTS

PRENATAL TESTS

What They Are,
Their Benefits and Risks,
and How to Decide Whether
to Have Them or Not

ROBIN J. R. BLATT

Introduction by
Wayne A. Miller, M.D., FACOG

VINTAGE BOOKS

A Division of Random House
New York

A Vintage Original, August 1988
First Edition

The information in this book is not presented as medical advice. The decision to choose or refuse to take prenatal tests is an individual matter. Neither the author nor the publisher can be responsible for these decisions or for any outcome that is a consequence of choosing or refusing these tests.

R.J.R. Blatt

Library of Congress Cataloging-in-Publication Data
Blatt, Robin J.R.
    Prenatal tests.
    "A Vintage original."
    Bibliography: p.
    Includes index.
    1. Prenatal diagnosis.   I. Title.
RG628.B53 1988   618.2'2   87-40546
ISBN 0-394-75887-0 (pbk.)

Page 259 constitutes an extension of this copyright page.

Manufactured in the United States of America

10 9 8 7 6 5 4 3 2 1

For Hannah and Gideon,
my children, my inspiration

Contents

Acknowledgments

Bearing witness to the physical, emotional, and spiritual effects of prenatal genetic tests has been an ethical odyssey compelling me to write this book. It is written with deep respect for all pregnant women and with gratitude to the men and women who shared with me the feelings that led them to choose or refuse prenatal testing.

These acknowledgments are a gesture of thanks to those who have been especially important to the development of this book. I am, however, grateful to more people than I can acknowledge in this space.

I thank my editor, Charlotte Mayerson, who appreciated the significance of this book when it was still an idea. Ruth Hubbard encouraged me to put pen to paper. She has been a continued source of support and wisdom. I am grateful to her for comments on the manuscript in its original handwritten form, and drafts thereafter. Discussions with her and Rita Arditti, Terry Goldberg, Laurie Jefferson, Shelley Minden, Elizabeth Noble, Marsha Saxton, Judy Norsigian, Nachama Wilker, Denise Karuth, and others involved in the formation of the Women and Reproductive Technology Group of the Committee for Responsible Genetics were inspirational. I am also thankful to the feminist writers whose work and guidance has enlightened me, in particular, Barbara Katz-Rothman, Dr. Michelle Harrison, and Nancy Wainer Cohen.

Several other colleagues, with whom I have shared concerns about prenatal tests, provided helpful criticisms of the manuscript. I am especially grateful for the thoughtful comments of

Dr. Wayne A. Miller, Dr. Allen Crocker, Marsha Lanes, and Adrienne Asch.

For many different kinds of teachings, I thank Betsy Anderson, Raphael Colb, Diane Dickey, Paula Haddow, Julie Hobbs, Eve Nichols, Dr. Jerry Kennedy, Pamela Painter, Rayna Rapp, Sarah Rosenfield, the Shalev family, Sally Whelan. I also thank my brother, Harvey Rosenfield, who has instructed me in many ways.

Certain experiences shape one's life and thoughts. Such are my feelings about my own prenatal care and two home births. The support of my midwife, Sloane Crawford, and Vicki Maclean, Dr. Linda Cooper, Harriette Hartigan, and Dr. Ronald Marcus will forever be remembered. I also acknowledge the young women, Amy Mace, Evelyn Bunker, and Kara Day, for tending my children during the gestation of this book.

To my husband, Chuck, I offer my love and appreciation for his sterling comments during all stages of this book and for making me keenly aware of the intensity of emotions associated with pregnancy and prenatal testing.

The last word of thanks, which really should have been the first, is for my mother, Sonya Carol, and for my father, Jack Rosenfield, who shaped both my genes and my environment.

Introduction
by Wayne A. Miller, M.D.

Any woman considering a pregnancy or currently pregnant is presented with a myriad of prenatal genetic tests that can significantly alter her approach to and progression of her pregnancy. *Prenatal Tests* by Robin J. R. Blatt is the first thorough consumer guide available on this topic. It is not only an accurate compendium of current technical information, but also a thoughtful account of the moral and ethical life decisions women and men must consider carefully before agreeing to tests to assess the genetic makeup of the unborn. It is this holistic approach that distinguishes *Prenatal Tests* from previously published books on this topic, and, in my view, makes it the best source and guide for pregnant women and their partners. Health care providers will also benefit from this book. It provides excellent insight into the perplexing and often conflicting parameters involved in their patients' decision-making processes.

The increase in medical knowledge over the past few decades has led to major new technologies in health care delivery. The rate at which this base of information and resultant applications has grown is astounding. In response, the basic manner in which medicine is practiced has changed. Specialists and subspecialists have proliferated as complex information and specialized techniques have been applied routinely in day-to-day medical care. Primary care providers have found it impossible to remain proficient in all areas. The attention paid to medical advances by the electronic and print media has also had a major effect on the manner in which new medical discoveries are disseminated. A decade ago, it was common for it to take a few years between the time that a new procedure or technology was first reported and the time it became familiar to the public and an accepted part of medical practice. Today, the press often headlines scientific reports before the information is even available to medical practitioners. The nature of reporting tends to simplify and overstate the "discovery," with the result that the public believes an experimental procedure or preliminary finding is established and readily available and applicable.

In no field of medicine have new technologies and information had a more pronounced effect than in the area of reproductive medicine and medical genetics. From planning a conception to delivery of the fetus, a woman and her partner are faced with multiple choices regarding application of available technologies. Some are actively promoted by health care providers, either from the belief that they are medically indicated and beneficial or in response to societal pressures that demand a "perfect" outcome to every pregnancy. Others are promoted through the lay press, friends, and family. Often the argument presented is that if the technology is available it should be used. Prospective parents may be bewildered and confused as to the necessity and validity of the procedures proposed or applied. Too often I have seen a couple accept a test or procedure without knowledge of its aim or potential consequences. Unfortunately, I have also seen couples who, because of fear or insufficient information, have rejected prenatal testing, with devastating outcomes they would have preferred to avoid. The rapid proliferation of technologies has spawned the expected naysayers who urge women to return pregnancy to medieval times by shunning all technology and modern interventions. Neither approach is valid. Available knowledge and technologies should be evaluated and a decision made, in concert with one's health care provider, as to the proper course of action in any given situation. Consumers and health professionals alike need to understand the balance between changing medical philosophies, the application of new technologies, and personal philosophies and needs. A good communication process throughout the prenatal care relationship is paramount to a healthy decision-making process.

This is the basic premise of Robin J. R. Blatt's book, *Prenatal*

Tests. It provides an accurate, up-to-date, and complete description of the various prenatal genetic tests available, a valid appraisal of their benefits, risks, limitations, and alternatives, and a framework for decision-making that patients can use given the presented information. Thoughtful treatment is given to the major genetic defects and congenital anomalies that are identified by prenatal genetic tests. Understanding the significance of these disorders is clearly the starting point from which most individuals would be expected to formulate their decision as to whether or not to utilize prenatal genetic testing, yet it is often overlooked by most other sources providing information on this subject. Similarly, excellent attention is given to the consequences of the decisions made and their physical, financial, and emotional effect on the individual, her family, and friends. Support mechanisms are identified and suggestions made for approaches to family and friends' questions for any decision or potential outcome.

This is not a medical textbook. The factual information presented is accurate and should provide sufficient background for a couple to interact with their health care provider when the question of prenatal genetic testing arises. I cannot emphasize enough one of Ms. Blatt's major points: Find a medical care provider whom you trust and with whom you can openly discuss your questions and concerns. If the guidelines presented in *Prenatal Tests* are followed, an informed decision regarding the application of any prenatal genetic test that is acceptable, comfortable, and correct should be within the grasp of any consumer.

The true significance of *Prenatal Tests* is that it goes beyond the descriptive details about prenatal genetic tests and their benefits and risks. It stimulates careful thought and questioning, incorporating personal values and needs in the decision-making process, offering techniques that will guide individuals to search within themselves for the answer to the question to test or not to test.

Wayne A. Miller, M.D., FACOG, Obstetrician/Geneticist. Assistant Professor of Pediatrics (Genetics), Harvard Medical School Director, Prenatal Diagnostic Center, Lincoln, Massachusetts.

BOOK ONE

Decisions of Early Pregnancy

1

Prenatal Genetic Testing— an Overview

THIS BOOK WAS WRITTEN ESPECIALLY FOR YOU IF . . .

- You are thinking of having prenatal testing—maternal serum alpha-fetoprotein screening (MSAFP), fetal ultrasound, amniocentesis, or chorionic villus sampling.

- You have been told that because of your age or some other factor, testing is essential.

- You want to consider all the risks and benefits before undergoing "routine" testing.

- You want to involve your partner in your pregnancy-related decisions.

- You believe that pregnancy is normal and natural, but you need some reinforcement for your inclination to refuse prenatal testing.

- You are interested in learning some unbiased facts about commonly discussed genetic disorders and birth defects.

- You want to know specific questions to ask your health care provider before you consent to or refuse any prenatal testing.

• You want to claim your own pregnancy and make informed decisions.

Like buying a layette or taking childbirth classes, prenatal genetic screening has become a ritual of modern pregnancy. Because the technology is there, though most babies are born healthy, more and more women are having genetic tests to screen for abnormalities in the developing fetus.* The current tests included in the "prenatal genetic testing package" are the maternal serum alpha-fetoprotein screening test, fetal ultrasound, amniocentesis, chorionic villus sampling, and, a recent addition, the percutaneous umbilical blood sampling test. Each of these medical and/or surgical procedures, with varying degrees of accuracy, confronts us with the prospect of discovering the genetic blueprint of our unborn baby. Pregnant women must now learn the vocabulary of a high-tech pregnancy. They must evaluate the risks and benefits of each test to both themselves and their unborn, decide which prenatal tests, if any, to undergo, and deal with the issue of how they will respond to the test results when they get them.

THE ORIGINS OF PRENATAL TESTING

Obviously, pregnancy itself is nothing new. The science of pregnancy is, though. Attempts to understand and control the mystery of the female body, as well as crude tests to predict fetal sex, date back to early civilizations. Ancient soothsayers tried to identify fetal sex by examining body contours. One test to determine the sex of the unborn involved a tribunal assessment of a pregnant woman's shape: If she was carrying "high," she was carrying a girl. If she was carrying "low," she was carrying a boy. Trinkets,

---

*Throughout this book I use the words "embryo," "fetus," "unborn," and "baby" interchangeably. It is not my intention to promote personhood of the fetus by interchanging this terminology. I have chosen this approach because women in most cultures refer to potential offspring as a "baby."

charms, and other gadgets were used to try to solve mysteries of inheritance. However, despite the long history of prenatal screening efforts, most of the technology that we accept today as "safe and justifiable for use in pregnancy" has been developed only during the past twenty years.

It wasn't until the late 1960s that geneticists overcame the mystery surrounding the "liquor and contents" of the womb. They were able to obtain cells from the developing baby *in utero* by withdrawing fluid from the uterus through a fine needle in a process called amniocentesis. When studied in the laboratory, these cells were found to reflect the genetic status of the fetus. In 1968 the first fetus with Down syndrome was diagnosed prior to birth.

Fetal ultrasound, another new prenatal technology that gained momentum in the 1960s, provides a window to the womb, allowing doctors to see the developing baby, to learn about growth and development *in utero*, and to identify certain variations in the maturation process.

The maternal serum alpha-fetoprotein screening test, developed in the 1970s, is a blood test that identifies women who may have an increased chance of having babies with open neural tube disorders, such as spina bifida. This test has been adapted to screen for fetuses with Down syndrome, and after only a few years of research, this controversial prenatal screening test has become a routine part of almost every woman's prenatal care plan.

Chorionic villus sampling (CVS) is another addition to the genetic testing package of early pregnancy. This test was originally designed to predict the sex of the unborn. It originated in China as part of a population-control program that almost invariably meant that female fetuses were aborted. Today, applications of chorionic villus sampling are being developed to examine the genetic makeup of the fetus in the third month of pregnancy. Although still highly experimental, many clinicians around the world see it as a revolutionary test that will soon replace amniocentesis.

Percutaneous umbilical blood sampling (PUBS) is the latest in prenatal testing technology. This procedure involves guiding a needle into the blood vessels within the umbilical cord to take a sample of fetal blood for genetic analysis.

Prenatal screening tests were originally designed for use with "high risk" women, those with an increased chance of delivering offspring with an "abnormal" condition. Traditionally, this definition included individuals with a family history of an inherited condition, parents who had a previous child with a specific disability, women who were at an advanced age or who had a medical condition that could affect fetal health, and individuals of certain ethnic backgrounds. However, medical dogma and perceptions of risk change along with the social and political climate. The definition of what constitutes medical and genetic risk also changes. New complicated classification systems categorize women as being at low risk, moderate risk, or high risk. Once pregnancy is put into a "risk" category, it is hard not to find some reason to test. Therefore, the number of women "eligible" or advised to undergo prenatal genetic screening procedures continually increases. As a result, many women are beginning to wonder: How has prenatal genetic screening suddenly become routine in pregnancy?

OUR CULTURE, TECHNOLOGY, AND PREGNANCY

The routine application of prenatal screening and diagnosis stems from a variety of social as well as medical causes. As high-tech genetic research proliferates, there has been expanded media coverage about birth defects and genetic diseases. The publicity about the rising incidence of genetic and environmental causes of disabilities has generated a condition of national anxiety among pregnant women. New methods of prenatal detection are being developed in response to this anxiety, though in some instances the technologies are developed first and then women begin to worry about a new aspect of their baby's health.

Although the process of being pregnant is the same as it's always been, our perception of our own body's competence has changed. Many modern women doubt their body's natural ability to create a healthy baby and, as a result, subject themselves to one or a combination of prenatal tests—each with its inherent risks— to reassure themselves that "everything is fine." Harvard biology professor Ruth Hubbard examines the implications of new prenatal technologies and their effects on pregnant women in her article, "Prenatal Courage Is Not Enough: Some Hazards of Childbearing in the 80s" (in the book *Test-Tube Women*). She points out that too many women gratefully accept the intrusions of insufficiently tested prenatal technology.

Another reason for the increased use of prenatal testing is that many women are postponing pregnancy until a later age. They belong to a generation of baby boomers of thirty to forty years old that is delaying pregnancy because of careers, advanced education, late marriages, treatable infertility, or financial concerns. Recently, advanced maternal age has become a topic of widespread interest. For example, there is a common belief that women over thirty-five run a higher risk of having a baby with certain disabilities, such as Down syndrome. Many women, conditioned to believe this is true, are asking for the tests with little inquiry.

Most women have wondered sometime during pregnancy, "Will my baby be healthy?" Now that prenatal tests are available and seem to answer this question, some of us are experiencing the "perfect baby" syndrome. We want to know as much as possible. If something is "wrong," some women want to terminate the pregnancy and try again. Access to safe abortions also allows women to decide whether or not to carry a fetus to term. This option has expanded the limits of women's choices during pregnancy and may account for the increased use of this technology.

Probably the most important factor contributing to the "perfect baby" syndrome and the general use of prenatal tests is our fears about people with disabilities. For centuries superstition and speculation have been used to explain children born with variations. We tend to have trouble accepting someone who is not "normal." Prenatal testing and the option of aborting an imperfect fetus have been likened to the eugenics movement: they are a means to improve the human race by getting rid of "undesira-bles." Although principles of eugenics may be intrinsic to prena-tal testing, the flip side is that these tests can offer women a choice to *have* the baby as well as to decline to do so.

The widespread availability of prenatal tests is analogous in some ways to the widespread availability of antibiotics. People often take antibiotics for colds when, in fact, they don't help. Antibiotics are a specific remedy intended for specific bacteria, just as most prenatal tests are intended for detecting *specific* con-ditions. Contrary to what many women believe, normal prenatal testing results do not *guarantee* a perfect baby at birth. At all stages, prenatal and postnatal, there is a chance of developing some sort of disability. And even if there were tests for every known condition, disabilities would never be eliminated. There will always be genetic changes. This is part of nature and evolu-tion.

There are also political reasons for the increasing use of prena-tal testing. Doctors fear malpractice suits; litigation is, in fact, on the rise. The American College of Obstetricians and Gynecolo-gists periodically releases "liability alerts" to obstetric health care providers, advocating the defensive use of prenatal tests to dimin-ish malpractice liability. Doctors are doing everything possible to avoid lawsuits.

There are also political lobbyists and organizations whose mis-sion is to stress the importance of preventing birth defects and to advocate the use of prenatal testing. As sophisticated scientific techniques are developed, new programs and subspecialties, such as genetic counseling and clinical and laboratory genetics, have evolved. Government funding of public health programs also pro-motes the use of these tests through the prolific publication of bulletins, official recommendations, and the sponsoring of legis-lation that ultimately affects how technology is used.

State governments encourage the development of biomedical technology because it is a boon to the local economy in terms of more business, more jobs, more taxes, more money. Industrial parks are being designed so that corporations doing genetic-engi-neering research or prenatal testing product development can have a world of their own in which to work. Little, if any, attention is given to the social, ethical, and health implications of the technology.

Economic forecasters predict that biotechnology firms which produce and market genetic technology will prosper. According to a recent survey, total laboratory revenues from genetic testing in the United States were $250 million in 1986 and are expected to reach $550 million in 1990. More than half of these revenues result from prenatal testing. Many of the prenatal tests appear to be inspired by academic or corporate entrepreneurs rather than by consumer need or demand. The promise of financial savings is another motivation for the widespread use of prenatal screening. Certain organizations use cost/benefit analyses to demonstrate the price of raising a disabled child versus the routine use of prenatal-screening tests. Since every disability is variable and no one really knows what it costs to raise an able-bodied child, these types of predictions are almost useless.

Finally, once expensive prenatal equipment becomes part of a doctor's office equipment, s/he may be motivated to use it, whether it is necessary or not. This is done to justify both the cost of the equipment and the rationale for buying it in the first place.

PUBLIC PERCEPTIONS OF SCIENCE

Sometimes the results of scientific meetings are published in newspapers and taken as new medical truths, even though the data may be incomplete, insufficiently supported, or even misinterpreted. In other instances, important findings take a long time to be incorporated into medical practice. For example, after a conference in 1983 on ultrasound many physicians were still unaware of the report or recommendations that ultrasound should not be routinely applied to every woman during pregnancy. Instead of the expected decrease, statistics demonstrate that the use of ultrasound continues to rise.

By the end of the decade, prenatal genetic testing will become an integral part of obstetric health care. A Presidential Ethics Commission report, "Screening and Counseling for Genetic Conditions," has already recommended that the practice of limiting amniocentesis to women over thirty-five is outdated and suggests that this test and others be made available to all pregnant women. The report represents a better-safe-than-sorry attitude.

The widespread application of genetic tests raises serious questions about experimentation on women, disability rights, and when life begins. Who is the patient—a pregnant woman or her fetus? Should genetic testing be voluntary or mandatory? Who should have access to the tests and their findings? What should be done with abnormal results? These are important and complex issues, yet they are being decided by a few scientists and governmental agencies with little consumer input.

For pregnant women today, there are several questions to consider: What are the implications of using methods and products that are still under investigation? Who should determine what tests a pregnant woman should undergo? Since no prenatal test can guarantee its results with 100 percent accuracy, how do you make the decision to choose or refuse prenatal testing? Before you decide, how do you know in advance how you would feel about having a baby with a disability?

A WOMAN'S DECISION

Because a complex web of medical, social, political, and economic forces support the use of prenatal testing, many women believe they no longer have a choice when it comes to applying one or a combination of these tests to their pregnant bodies. But it is important that they recognize that the decision to choose or refuse prenatal testing is still their own personal prerogative.

Recently, a friend asked, "Isn't it wiser for a woman to just put herself in the hands of the doctor (who, after all, is the expert), without questioning the recommendations for prenatal care and genetic testing?" "Absolutely not," I replied. I believe it is important for women to decide carefully about prenatal testing. Women have a right to know about the tests and the issues they will have to confront as well as the right to determine what will be done to their bodies. Because most women have little or no understanding of the medical art of genetics, it's important that they educate themselves and that they choose a prenatal care provider whom they can talk to and trust.

If you allow your doctor to order an ultrasound to see how far along you are in the pregnancy, or to schedule an amniocentesis only because of your age, you are agreeing that you have no choice. This also means that you don't have to take responsibility for having made a "wrong" decision if something unexpected happens, or if the test does not reap the hoped-for results.

Not to make decisions in pregnancy means that you may feel like a victim rather than the master of your own fate. If you enter the high-technology process without carefully considering the issues, you may find yourself in a situation that you did not anticipate, one that could result in a great deal of unhappiness.

In contrast, if you take the opportunity to gain self-awareness and carefully explore the benefits and risks of each prenatal test, you will be making conscious decisions about your pregnancy. You will be taking responsibility for yourself and will feel empowered by your own knowledge and inner strength.

HOW TO USE THIS BOOK

Most of the advice pregnant women get tells them who "should" have prenatal testing, without letting them make their own decisions. The usefulness of these tests is often overemphasized. They are commonly portrayed as safe, and many of the risks or mistakes that occur are not adequately described.

I hope that this book will support you in a self-help approach to decision-making. The information is here. Use it to talk with your partner and your health care provider and then make the best decision for yourself.

The early chapters of this book describe the individual prenatal tests along with possible benefits and risks to you and your unborn baby. Later sections provide up-to-date information to help you evaluate whether you have any special risk factors for having a baby with a disability. With this information you can decide which prenatal tests, if any, would be most appropriate for you.

Finally, I've gathered the experiences and wisdom of women

who have made a variety of pregnancy choices. Though their names have been changed in the narrative, their voices are authentic and come out of my own years of interaction with women faced with making prenatal genetic decisions.

Even if you feel that you have already made your decision about prenatal testing, review these steps:

1. Face the decision.

2. Learn about prenatal genetic tests.

3. Envision your options.

4. Make the decision.

This review of the decision-making process will help you recognize whether your first decision is really your best decision.

I have written this book with deep concern for women who are exploring the possibilities of having prenatal tests. It is not intended to give medical advice or to provide complete information, because of the unique differences in each woman and in each pregnancy. Instead, it is designed to provide information that will help you make thoughtful decisions about prenatal health care. I hope the book will heighten your awareness of the opportunities open to you during your pregnancy and put pregnancy power where it belongs—with you!

2 | Decisions of Early Pregnancy

Congratulations. You have decided to take control of your life and make some important decisions about applying genetic technology to your pregnancy. Think of your decision as an act of love—for you and your unborn baby—and as a way of gaining freedom from outside controls to do what you feel is right.

Shortly after you begin this process of decision-making, you will feel better and anxiety about your pregnancy will lessen. You will become an active participant throughout your pregnancy journey. And above all, you will enjoy an enormous surge of self-confidence that will stay with you for the rest of your life. Perhaps you are wondering: Doctor or midwife? To screen or not to screen? To ultrasound or not to ultrasound? To amnio or not to amnio? These are among the decisions of early pregnancy.

If you are undecided about whether or not to have prenatal tests, or if your health care provider routinely orders tests without enough consultation with you, remember that taking part in the decision-making process is healthy. There is no universally correct decision. Whether you choose or refuse to have prenatal tests depends on your unique situation, but keep in mind that most babies are born healthy.

HOW THE SYMPTOMS OF EARLY PREGNANCY AFFECT OUR DECISIONS

Many women find it difficult to explore the reasons for choosing or refusing prenatal testing in the early weeks of pregnancy. During this time, tension, nausea, and fatigue are among the normal emotional and physical symptoms that often appear. These symptoms frequently distract them from thinking about whether or not they want prenatal testing. One woman, reflecting on her early pregnancy, said, "If I feel this sick, something must be wrong." This is not so. It is important to be aware of the physical and emotional changes that are normal in early pregnancy. (The bibliography lists books that describe these natural changes.) Once you understand and possibly have eased some of your early pregnancy discomforts, you will be in a better position to focus attention on the decision to choose or refuse prenatal testing.

THE "NEW" PREGNANCY EXPERIENCE

The ancient mystery of pregnancy that once bound women from generation to generation has abruptly been made more complex by modern scientists whose technology has changed the experience. Today's women are of the first generation to confront the dilemmas posed by the information prenatal technology provides. As they begin to make choices, they need to keep in mind that their goals and assumptions and those of medical researchers may not always be the same. Researchers want all the information they can get about the unborn baby. They rely on new technologies for this purpose. Women, on the other hand, may choose to decline forecasts that can be ambiguous or about which they can or will do nothing. Or there may be things they just don't want to know—like the sex of the baby. As a result of these "forced choices," many of them connected with the prenatal tests, uncertainty and anxiety are now becoming accepted as a normal part of early pregnancy.

Another effect of technology is that often the fetus is treated as the patient. Many obstetricians are becoming "fetal doctors," and this is having a strong legal impact. Some women who have not done what the doctor recommended have been put in jail for "fetus abuse." Other women have been made to feel extremely guilty when their lives make it impossible, for example, for them to stay in bed for their entire pregnancy. In general, women's needs are being superseded by those of the unborn.

Perhaps the most significant impact of prenatal technology has to do with a pregnant woman's relationship to her unborn baby. Studies of attachment have demonstrated that bonding—the so-called loving relationship that may develop between a woman and her fetus—can occur during early pregnancy. Today, however, many pregnant women are experiencing the "nonattachment syndrome." Although some women say that seeing a baby on ultrasound for example, hastens bonding, recent interviews have revealed that if women know they will be having prenatal testing, they keep an emotional distance until after they receive the test results and know whether or not the baby is "all right." According to sociologist Barbara Katz-Rothman, in her book *Tentative Pregnancy,* some women don't want to become attached until they know whether they will be having a baby or an abortion. I have talked with many women who completely shut out the fetus emotionally. One woman who decided to have prenatal testing said, "I couldn't feel my baby move until after my prenatal tests, when I was told my baby was okay. I am sad now that I ignored any hints of its existence for the first sixteen weeks." The connection between biology and emotion is fairly well documented. It appears that there is a meshing of maternal and fetal rhythms and responses. If a woman is tense and fearful about fetal health, it may be that her emotional-hormonal response can powerfully affect the baby's environment.

There is, however, a different approach to pregnancy, one that permits you to develop a closeness with your growing baby no matter what the outcome of prenatal tests, if you decide to have them. It is an aspect of a new way of thinking of our health and well-being, a holistic approach.

DEVELOPING A HOLISTIC APPROACH

Holistic health care recognizes that all parts of a person are interdependent and strives to treat the entire person. In obstetrics, this type of care differs from the traditional medical approach in which mother, uterus, and fetus are treated as separate entities. A united mind-body-spirit perspective assumes that the relationship of mind and body, of woman and fetus, is not divisible. Prenatal plans can also take this into account.

Applying a holistic approach to prenatal testing means you can explore all aspects of your physical, emotional, and spiritual self and can take responsibility for the decisions you make during pregnancy. You do not have to alienate yourself from your baby or the changes taking place in your body.

If you want to minimize the divisiveness that technology can create, talk to your unborn baby every day, share your feelings and concerns, tell your baby you love her/him no matter what happens. It may be healthy for you to communicate and develop a relationship with your baby, even if you plan to have prenatal testing and would choose an abortion upon receiving an abnormal diagnosis. One woman recalls her enjoyment in the early months of pregnancy. "When my baby moved, it felt like a tickle from my insides. After the amniocentesis, I was told that my baby had Down syndrome. Just as I received this news I felt that sensation again. I was stunned. I felt like I knew this being inside me and that we would be able to survive her disability."

Another woman who made a different choice also was pleased that she had established an early relationship with her unborn child. "I was attuned to what felt like my 'baby' and not my 'fetus,' as the doctors were calling her. I could feel every flutter, and I called her my little 'butterfly.' When I learned that my baby had an irreversible genetic disorder, I chose to have an abortion. Even though it was the most painful decision of my life, I still have memories of my baby being real to me."

PREPARING TO CHOOSE OR REFUSE PRENATAL TESTING

Making a conscious decision about prenatal testing is one of your many gifts to yourself, your unborn baby, and your family. In addition, understanding your feelings and thoughts about prenatal testing:

- gives you an opportunity to learn about yourself.

- allows you to keep control of your pregnancy.

- gives you the tools to assess the physical risks of the test to you and your unborn baby.

- gives you pride in assuming responsibility.

- increases the probability that you will make the most of your choice.

- builds skills for future decision-making.

You will need to look at the objective facts as well as within yourself to decide whether or not to have prenatal tests. The more comfortable you are with your decision, the more comfortable you will be with your pregnancy.

SEEKING SUPPORT FOR PRENATAL DECISIONS

Although the decision to choose or refuse to take prenatal tests is ultimately yours, you do not need to make it alone. Ideally, both parents who participated in the decision to bear a child should be fully involved. If you exclude your partner now, it might lead to a later lack of involvement. I have found that involving partners in prenatal care checkups, as well as in the prenatal testing procedures, can provide a special form of psychological support and can help make pregnancy a shared experience. In fact, some "pregnant partners" say they experience pregnancy physically, emotionally, and spiritually. Physically, partners report similar feelings such as nausea and weight gain. Emotionally, they may experience restlessness, anxiety, and a similar concern for the baby's health.

Unfortunately, many women feel they don't receive enough support during pregnancy, either for what they are experiencing or for the complex decisions regarding prenatal testing. Some women do not have a partner to share their concerns; others can't discuss the issues with the father of the child.

Whether you are living alone and considering single parenthood, or you are in a relationship, choose someone (husband, lover, mother, sister, friend) to share your plans for pregnancy and birth. This person can accompany you during prenatal care visits, during prenatal testing (if you choose to have it), during an abortion (if that becomes your choice), or when you give birth.

You're both making a commitment that requires time, energy, and skill. The following guidelines may be helpful when you discuss prenatal testing together.

• Consult your partner about a good time and place to talk. Disagreements frequently occur because one of you is tired or not feeling well or because the place isn't private enough. Make a date and keep it.

• If either of you feels any frustration or anger toward the other, try to clear the air. Express your love and support for each other.

• Tell your partner you are going to make a conscious, careful decision about prenatal testing and that you need his or her commitment to this process. Both of you will need to educate yourselves in order to make a decision together.

• Describe your situation and your feelings. Let your partner know how these choices are affecting you physically, emotionally, and spiritually.

• Make a list of your expectations for the other person and ask your partner to make his or her own list. Share these lists.

• Listen to your partner's feelings. We often hear only what we want to hear. Try to stay in the present moment and listen.

• Both of you should read this book, compare notes, and then discuss your individual beliefs about prenatal testing.

• Before finishing your discussion, try to come to an agreement, even if it's temporary, until the next time you talk. Set a date to continue your conversation.

• Ask your partner for love and support while you are undergoing this process. Cooperation brings peace and harmony to both of you.

Not all partners will be able to give you the support you need. Some may want to direct the course of action, others would rather leave the decisions about prenatal testing up to you, your doctor, or your midwife.

In the final analysis, it is your right to decide whether or not to undergo medical and surgical prenatal tests. This conclusion is not meant to reinforce the mistaken assumption that mothering is more important than fathering or that children are only a woman's concern, but to emphasize that each prenatal test procedure involves risks to a woman's health, and a commitment, usually the woman's, to care for the child she bears. Therefore, if you feel pressured into prenatal testing or if you have to make this decision alone, consider seeking outside help—from a prenatal counselor or a support group.

Your decision about prenatal testing will eventually be based on individual circumstances, such as your personal "risk factors," your attitude about disability, your support system, and the influence of the health care provider you choose to see for prenatal care.

YOUR PRENATAL CARE

Prenatal care is the health care that a woman receives before her baby is born. There is a new theory that women who start prenatal care early in their pregnancies tend to have fewer problems and deliver healthier babies. However, prenatal care does not automatically result in a healthier baby. The outcome of pregnancy is influenced by a combination of your genetic profile, your environment, and chance. It also depends on your health before and during early pregnancy and may be influenced by whom you see for prenatal care.

The medical community has placed new emphasis on prepregnancy or preconception planning. Some hospitals now offer prepregnancy planning classes, and some practitioners suggest that both potential parents meet with them before conception to assess their health and review their personal and family histories. During this meeting, a provider may review immunization records, adjust any medications or medical treatments, and discuss nutrition and other aspects of health that may affect an unborn baby. This meeting can also be used to identify the chances of passing on a particular inherited disorder and to describe available genetic screening tests.

The basic theory behind preconception planning is that early care is the best way to discover and treat a potential problem. Such programs do give some women a sense of reassurance that they are doing everything possible to have a healthy baby. The problem is, that though it's not clear that this kind of preparation is necessary, the fact that it is available makes those women who get pregnant without preconception counseling worry that they will not have the "optimum baby."

There is no doubt that prenatal care and health education are important. We have only to look at how many low-birth-weight babies are born to mothers who don't get diet and health counseling. What is much more questionable is the current trend toward a highly technological, medically supervised pregnancy. The women's health movement fought hard to put reproductive decision-making and health care into women's hands. There is a danger that the new, highly medicalized prenatal techniques will undermine that control. To prevent that, women need to learn all they can about the new prenatal techniques and to be active participants in deciding how and when to use them.

THE HEALTH CARE PROVIDERS

There are many kinds of health care professionals who may be qualified to care for you during your pregnancy, labor and delivery, and the period after birth. Since you are asking this person to assist you on a very important journey, be sure to choose your provider carefully. The following are health professionals who deal with the special needs of women in pregnancy.

An obstetrician-gynecologist (OB-GYN) is a medical doctor, certified by the American College of Obstetricians and Gynecologists, who is trained to provide medical and surgical care to women. Obstetricians provide mainly pregnancy care, while gynecologists provide general care for women's reproductive systems. Only licensed obstetricians are trained to perform surgical prenatal diagnostic procedures such as chorionic villus sampling and amniocentesis.

A perinatalogist—or high-risk doctor—is an obstetrician who specializes in the care of women who may face special problems during pregnancy.

A family practitioner (FP) is a medical doctor who specializes in health care for all family members. Family practitioners are prepared to provide obstetric and gynecologic care, but refer women with complicated problems or who choose prenatal testing to an obstetrician-gynecologist for an evaluation.

A general practitioner (GP) is a medical doctor who provides a wide variety of health care. Some general practitioners provide basic obstetric and gynecologic care but refer women to an obstetrician for prenatal testing.

A nurse practitioner (NP) is a registered nurse with advanced training in maternal and child health care. Some nurse practitioners act independently in providing pregnancy-related care, but refer women to a medical doctor for prenatal testing or if a complication arises. Many nurse practitioners practice with doctors to provide prenatal care and education.

A certified nurse-midwife (CNM) is a registered nurse who has graduated from an accredited midwifery program and who is trained to provide comprehensive health care to women and their babies from early pregnancy through labor, delivery, and after birth. Midwives support and manage a woman during labor, perform normal vaginal deliveries, and provide immediate aftercare both for a mother and the baby. They also offer counseling in areas such as breast-feeding, diet, parenting, and family planning. In some states, nurse-midwives practice independently; in other states they practice with a doctor. Nurse-midwives can help you understand your reasons for choosing or refusing prenatal testing. They can refer you to an obstetrician for prenatal testing or an evaluation if a complication arises.

A lay midwife is a person (with or without a traditional medical background) who provides the same type of care as a nurse-midwife.

As you choose the person who will provide you with regular prenatal care and guide you throughout delivery, consider whether you want a midwife or a doctor. They each have their advantages and disadvantages, and their education-related biases. Today, many women are choosing a "birthing team," where both a midwife and a doctor participate or back each other up.

THE RELATIONSHIP BETWEEN PRENATAL TECHNOLOGY AND YOUR PROVIDER

Most women make decisions about prenatal testing based on what their practitioner tells them. For that reason, you should consider what factors influence the advice your practitioner is likely to give you. The midwife or doctor's specialty, place of training and year of graduation, university affiliation, religious affiliation, and geographic location are all important. For example, a doctor working in a university-affiliated teaching hospital would have access to and would more readily apply high technology to pregnancy, whereas a physician or midwife who attends births in a birthing center or at home may not. Midwives do seem to be less "intervention-oriented" than physicians. Choose the practitioner whose philosophy is closest to your own. Many women assume that the sex of the doctor will influence the approach to prenatal care, but this is not necessarily so. Most women doctors share the same training and attitudes of their male colleagues.

SELECTING YOUR PROVIDER

Once you've decided what your needs are, look for the provider and place of care with which you feel most comfortable. Do you want your provider to be a doctor or midwife, older or younger, serious or with a sense of humor, male or female, white or a person of color? What language do you want your provider to speak? Good prenatal care takes place when there is trust and communication. Explain the type of professional you are looking for and ask for names from your regular health care provider, as well as from neighbors, friends, and relatives who share your views about life and who have recently had a baby in your community. Find out specifically why that person likes or dislikes the practitioner. Her reasons may be different from yours.

You can call the midwifery department of a local hospital or a nurse on a labor and delivery ward or in the newborn nursery and ask for a few names of doctors and midwives. You can also call your local childbirth-education group. Try to get the advice of an independent childbirth organization rather than one that is part of a hospital and must refer you to their own professionals. La Leche League, an organization that supports breast-feeding, has networks of pregnant and parenting women throughout the country.

The next step is for you to interview the person you're considering as your provider. It's your job to find out all you can about this person and also to communicate your needs, goals, and expectations. Many of us feel undeserving of a busy doctor's time or assume that the midwife is too occupied to bother with details that may be important to us. We don't want to look uninformed or talk too much, or we're afraid the practitioner will be insulted if we ask about his or her credentials. Remember, you are paying for information and advice and you have a responsibility to yourself and your baby to find the best person.

Write down your questions ahead of time so you don't forget

them. Ask about anything that is unclear and repeat the answers back to the provider in your own words. Never be afraid to ask your provider to translate medical terms into language you can understand.

If your partner can join you in the office visit or get on an extension phone if you are calling your provider, one of you can take notes while the other one asks questions. Or use a tape recorder. Some of the things you may want to explore include the following:

- Your practitioner's view of pregnancy.

- Your practitioner's perspective on the use of technology during pregnancy and childbirth.

- Is the provider board certified or just board eligible by a particular professional organization? (Being certified does not guarantee excellence; it does mean that the provider has taken an approved program and passed a certifying exam.)

There are many other questions to be asked and issues to be explored before you choose a prenatal health provider. Consult the appendix for the names of childbirth organizations and resources that will help you choose someone good.

From the point of view of prenatal testing, it is crucial that you ask your doctor how s/he practices. Does s/he have an ultrasound machine in the office and use it routinely? Does s/he do the amniocentesis her/himself, or will you be referred to a specialized genetics center for these services? Is there formal genetic counseling before you are asked to decide about prenatal screening or diagnostic testing? Who actually does the counseling—the doctor, nurse, midwife, genetic counselor, or the scheduling secretary?

If your doctor does prenatal genetic testing her/himself, be sure to ask questions about experience, skill, and training. If you are referred to a genetics center, ask the doctors there the same questions. No matter whom you see, you may also want to know what laboratory is used for routine tests and genetic studies. (See chapter 3 for information about the laboratory's role in prenatal testing.) For specific questions to ask whoever does the different procedures, see chapter 15. Before consenting to a particular procedure in early pregnancy, talk with your provider about the issues raised in the appropriate test chapter.

THE GENETICS PERSONNEL

If you are considering prenatal testing or genetic studies, or your pregnancy is interrupted by either a miscarriage or an abortion, there are other professionals you may be referred to who will have a role in your pregnancy experience.

A geneticist is a medical doctor (often an obstetrician or pediatrician) with advanced training in human genetics who can provide genetic counseling, order genetic studies or prenatal testing, interpret the tests, and, if possible, suggest treatment for persons with inherited conditions. There are also a number of laboratory-based geneticists who do research and hold Ph.D.'s in human genetics.

A genetic counselor or genetic associate has a master's degree in human genetics and counseling. Most genetic counselors work for geneticists, providing education, pretest counseling, and support. Chapter 14 describes genetic counseling in more detail.

An embryologist is a medical doctor specializing in fetal growth and development. Some embryologists specialize in studying the effects of teratogens (harmful substances) that may interfere with fetal development.

A cytogenetic technologist is a professional who actually looks at and analyzes the genetic makeup of cells under a microscope in the laboratory.

A pathologist is a medical doctor who identifies pathology or disease in human tissue and who performs an autopsy/fetopsy.

LISTEN TO YOUR INNER VOICE

No matter whom you choose to provide your prenatal care, try to find someone who:

- supports your beliefs.

- takes time to do a thorough history.

- remembers your first and last names.

- is pleased for you about your pregnancy.

- encourages you to take responsibility.

- is relaxed and takes time to listen.

- does not overschedule.

- is not patronizing.

- is knowledgeable and stays current on prenatal testing.

- provides verbal reinforcement by saying everything looks fine when it does.

- tells you clearly and promptly when things appear to be going wrong.

- is honest about risks, benefits, and side effects of tests and treatments.

- explains her or his thinking and involves you in decision-making.

- is willing to negotiate.

- has had experience and training in prenatal testing or can refer you to a comprehensive genetic center if you choose to have any of these tests.

- inspires trust.

Read the test sections in this book carefully. Listen to your inner voice when making this important decision. Try to resist the urge to stay with a provider out of loyalty or habit. A good reputation, respect, and competence don't guarantee empathy. If at any time you are concerned about the care you are receiving, tell your provider. If there is a conflict or your concern goes unacknowledged, shop around. You are not obligated to remain with a provider with whom you have little in common. Conversely, a provider can refuse to care for you.

Weigh your reasons for staying with a practitioner against your reasons for wanting to change. Many women feel embarrassed because they have a personal relationship with their doctor. They fear it will be too complicated to find someone else as good or that they'll be seen as a troublemaker or that they won't get their medical records. Most of these worries are groundless. Remember, it's never too late to change health care providers. If you are dissatisfied with your provider's attitude or the care you are receiving during your pregnancy, imagine what it could be like during labor when you are more vulnerable and in need of support. If, in fact, your choice of provider is limited by your financial situation, or by where you live, try to find other people who will be able to give you emotional support and guidance.

The person you choose to provide prenatal care will play a crucial role in your making a decision about prenatal tests. If you respect that person, trust his or her judgments, and feel that s/he understands you, you will have created an optimum situation for what can be a fulfilling pregnancy experience.

YOUR FIRST PRENATAL CARE VISIT

During your first visit your provider should ask you questions about your life-style. Generally s/he will assess genetic and environmental risk factors, which include your family history, the stresses in your life, your social and emotional supports, your feelings about your pregnancy, your experience with parenting, and your home and work environment. Your nutritional status should also be explored. Adequate nutrition before conception and during pregnancy contributes to a healthy pregnancy. Prenatal education and counseling should always be tailored to your educational, linguistic, ethnic, and cultural background. If you need it, you should ask for written information so you can refer to it when you leave the doctor's office.

Your physical exam will probably include the following:

- A measurement of your height, weight, and blood pressure.

- An examination of your eyes, ears, nose, throat, and teeth.

- An examination of your heart, lungs, breasts, and abdomen.

- An internal examination (pelvic exam) of the size and position of your uterus.

Several laboratory tests may be performed:

- A pregnancy test to check for the hormone human chorionic gonadotrophin (HCG). This hormone can be detected in your blood within days after conception. Some providers will repeat this test, even if you have already done a urine test at home with an over-the-counter home-pregnancy test kit.

- Blood tests such as a hemoglobin (Hgb) and hematocrit (Hct) test to check for anemia or iron deficiency, or serum protein to check nutritional status. These tests are often repeated between the twenty-eighth and thirty-second weeks.

- Blood samples to determine your blood type (A, B, O, AB) and your Rhesus group (Rh factor), which will either be positive or negative. If you are Rh negative, your baby's father should also be tested (see p. 82).

- Antibody tests to check your immunity to infectious diseases such as rubella (German measles), measles, mumps, cytomegalovirus, toxoplasmosis, hepatitis, and possibly AIDS. Depending on your exposure, some of these tests may be repeated at different intervals during your pregnancy.

- Blood glucose tests to check for gestational diabetes (diabetes occurring only during pregnancy).

- Urine tests to check for sugar and protein in order to assess whether or not you have diabetes and to determine how well your kidneys function. These tests also check for the possibility of infection.

• A Pap smear of your cervix to screen for cancer, and a vaginal culture to check for sexually transmitted diseases such as chlamydia, gonorrhea, or genital herpes. A blood test will also be done to see if you have syphilis.

• Genetic screening tests to identify whether you have the potential to pass on an inherited disorder to your baby.

During an early prenatal visit, your provider may give you information about prenatal tests s/he thinks you will need. These tests are the subject of the remainder of this book. They include maternal serum alpha-fetoprotein (MSAFP) screening test, ultrasound, amniocentesis, chorionic villus sampling (CVS), percutaneous umbilical blood sampling (PUBS), and the newer reproductive technologies.

Ideally, early prenatal care should include discussion and advice about your pregnancy and the delivery rather than a quick check of your blood pressure and the size of your uterus. Now is the time for you and your provider to develop a plan of care tailored to your special needs. Ask your provider for extra visits if you want to discuss at greater length certain aspects of your pregnancy or the choices you will have to make.

The plan for your pregnancy should include a schedule of appointments with your primary provider. Nutrition and exercise needs should be a part of your plan as well as an estimate of how long you will stay on your job, who will attend your delivery, and what other specialists, if any, you will need to consult. Most important is to discuss as early as possible the plan for prenatal testing, if there is to be any.

CHOOSING OR REFUSING PRENATAL TESTING

In most states pregnant women have the legal right to choose or refuse prenatal testing. This book has been written to help you make that decision. It will tell you what each procedure is, the type of information it can and cannot provide, the risks to you and/or the baby, the possibility and meaning of ambiguous or inaccurate diagnoses, how to evaluate the results and decide what to do when given the options based on those results.

You have the following rights in regard to these tests:

- To choose or refuse prenatal testing no matter how old or in what stage of your pregnancy you are.

- To choose or refuse prenatal testing even if you know you won't have an abortion.

- To choose or refuse prenatal testing even if you know that you want a nonintervention, or home birth.

- To consider these issues whether you are single, married, or gay.

- To have your lover or friend receive the same respect usually given to a spouse or relative.

- To change your mind at any time in the prenatal testing process.

- To be treated respectfully and fairly by your provider.

- To examine your medical records.

- To know or not know the sex of your fetus.

- To be given all the findings of your tests even when they are of disputed importance.

- To have your privacy respected, including any discussion with your doctor, midwife, nurse, health worker, or health administrator.

- To have your name withheld from genetic registries or centralized data banks, unless you give permission.

- To have any reproductions of your ultrasound pictures or your chromosome studies withheld from publication or from being used in teaching, unless you give permission.

• To receive information about financial aid to help you pay the bills for prenatal testing and for courteous assistance in obtaining any money for which you may be eligible.

• To have a second opinion to satisfy yourself that you are getting the best diagnosis.

• To ask for clarification when you are in doubt.

• To know which laboratory is processing your blood, tissue, or amniotic fluid specimen, whether the laboratory participates in a proficiency testing program (external quality control), and how they rate in comparison with other laboratories.

3 | Practical Considerations

In the following chapters you will learn about prenatal genetic tests. With this knowledge you will be able to begin to assess your own pregnancy risks. Perhaps you will conclude that there are no specific genetic or environmental influences in your life that warrant your using prenatal testing, or perhaps you will feel that there are. Despite any "medical indications," you still have the choice to test or not to test. Before making this decision, it is important to learn more about each individual test and then to compare the risks of the procedures with your chances for having a baby with a disability.

In addition to the medical factors, there are some practical matters to consider when thinking about the tests.

TIMING PRENATAL TESTING

Pregnancy usually takes nine months, or forty weeks. Some women take a little longer to grow babies and some a little less. Generally speaking two weeks in either direction is normal.

These nine months are divided by professionals into trimesters of pregnancy. The first trimester includes months one to three; the second trimester, months three to six; the third, months six to nine. Until recently, most prenatal tests used to screen for birth defects were offered in the second trimester. Now, first and third trimester tests are also used for prenatal diagnosis. The timing can be seen in this chart. The tests are described in the following chapters.

TIMING PRENATAL TESTS

1–3 Months	3–6 Months	6–9 Months
CVS	MSAFP screening	Ultrasound
Ultrasound	Ultrasound	Amniocentesis
	Amniocentesis	PUBS
	PUBS	

Each of these tests has a "window," or a period of time, when it is considered safe and accurate. The timing of each test is based on the date of your last menstrual period (LMP), not when you conceived.

To calculate your LMP, note the first day of your last menstrual period. In a twenty-eight-day cycle, the probable date of conception is usually, but not always, two weeks after your LMP.

CALCULATING TEST DATES

Use a calendar and your LMP date to calculate when you might have the various prenatal tests. Then note them below:

1) Chorionic villus sampling (9–12 weeks after your LMP)
   _____

2) Maternal serum alpha-fetoprotein screening (16–18 weeks after your LMP) _____

3) Ultrasound (16–18 weeks after your LMP)
   _____

4) Amniocentesis (16–18 weeks after your LMP)
   _____ (Some doctors are doing early amnios between 12–14 weeks after your LMP.)

5) Percutaneous umbilical blood sampling (anywhere from 16–34 weeks after your LMP)
   _____

If you are strongly considering one or more of these tests, call your health care provider to schedule appointments. Often it is necessary to schedule prenatal testing far in advance because it frequently involves setting aside a special procedure room, arranging for equipment and personnel, and coordinating the laboratory services. If your provider does not perform the test her/himself, it may also take time to arrange for a referral to a specialist. Scheduling these tests in advance will give you some time to think about your choices. Remember, you can always change your mind at a later date.

THE DOMINO EFFECT

Many women undergo tests during pregnancy without knowing what choices the results might force them to consider. As you will see when we talk about the individual procedures, one test can lead to another. That means that you may have to make decisions you never have imagined. It also means you have to plan carefully so that tests are done at the time they're most effective. Your doctor might not explain the domino effect of this testing process since s/he may not want to worry you, or because it takes time to explain.

The genetic tests are usually given at the following times: ultrasound, throughout pregnancy for a variety of reasons, sixteenth to eighteenth week to screen for disabilities; chorionic villus sampling, eighth to twelfth week; MSAFP screening, sixteenth to eighteenth week; amniocentesis, sixteenth to eighteenth

week; and percutaneous umbilical sampling, eighteenth to forti-
eth week.

HEALTH INSURANCE

This is the time to think about the type of insurance coverage you
have and what services your policy covers. This differs from state
to state and according to market demand. Your geographic location, the technologies available, the pregnancy rate, and whether
there are requests for reimbursement from providers, subscri-
bers, and employers may determine whether or not certain genetic services will be covered. Some health insurance companies,
in deciding whether or not to include coverage for genetic services, base their decision on what gives them a competitive advantage in the marketplace.

If you are considering testing, you will want to know not only
which prenatal tests your insurance policy covers, but also what
will be covered as a result of the test findings. For example, if a
disability is identified and you decide to have an abortion, does
your policy cover "medically necessary abortions"? If you were
to learn your baby has a disability and you think you might carry
your baby to term, do you have adequate coverage for your baby's
potential special needs after birth?

Your insurance policy may not contain enough practical information nor clearly state which genetic tests or services are covered, and your health care provider may not know about your
particular policy.

In order to learn what prenatal tests are covered by your insurance policy, you might be able to obtain information from the
division of insurance in your state. Make a phone inquiry, but
don't be surprised if this is a frustrating process. The issue that
you might be raising, such as going out of state for a prenatal test,
may simply not have come up before or there may be no coverage. If you are dissatisfied with the response, you can appeal a
decision about coverage, although the steps may not always be
clear and the results may depend on who happens to review your
case.

Unfortunately, decisions on coverage for specific prenatal screening services that need to be reviewed or approved within the insurance company often come too late, after you have had to make the decision or have incurred the debt.

If you do not have health insurance, there may be government programs that will pay for prenatal tests. Unfortunately, as in the case of Medicaid, there are strict income requirements in order to qualify for this help. If you are concerned about coverage, ask your health care provider, a social worker connected to the clinic or hospital, or your company's benefits manager.

THE LABORATORY BEHIND THE SCENE

Most prenatal tests, with the exception of ultrasound, require laboratory services. Because there is such a wide variation in laboratory proficiency, you should be aware of some factors that can influence prenatal test results.

Until recently all prenatal specimens—blood, amniotic fluid, and tissue—were sent to a cytogenetics laboratory specifically for genetic studies. This type of lab was once limited to university-affiliated centers with research scientists overseeing laboratory procedures. Now, many commercial laboratories include genetic studies as only one component of their services. There are also highly specialized genetic laboratories, known as high-tech bio-technology labs, that compete with ordinary commercial labs and academic laboratory facilities. Some of these biotechnology labs are owned by cytogeneticists (M.D.'s or Ph.D.'s) who once worked in academic research institutions.

No matter which type of laboratory your provider uses, certain conditions within the lab can contribute to the overall accuracy of results. Test results, and, ultimately, the course of your pregnancy, can be influenced by the type of protocol being followed, who actually does the analysis and makes the interpretation, and the training and experience of the personnel.

INTERPRETING TEST RESULTS

Although interpretation of laboratory results is supposed to be the doctors' domain, laboratory protocol varies. Some laboratories call or mail test results to a provider, with a figure or result and their ranges of normal for their particular lab. The provider is expected to interpret the results. Other labs interpret the results and make recommendations for follow-up tests. In some instances a medical doctor or a cytogeneticist will do this work. In other instances it could be a laboratory technician or a biochemist. Obviously the expertise of the person who interprets laboratory results is crucial.

Your health care provider should inquire about and inform you of the results of the laboratory tests. The provider is still in many ways the commander-in-chief of prenatal care. It is, finally, his/her responsibility when laboratory tests are performed or reported negligently.

As more and more labs are starting to use automated machines and computers to process and interpret the specimens from prenatal tests, even more diligence will be required until this technology is perfected.

LABORATORY ACCURACY

Most state laboratory licensing bureaus monitor the quality of laboratory services, but unfortunately, performance requirements are not always enforced. Some labs that consistently have problems are still in operation.

In one instance, when a woman was tested to see if she carried a gene for Tay-Sachs disease, her blood sample was first sent to a commercial laboratory. Days later it was forwarded to a specialized Tay-Sachs screening lab. Four weeks later, she called the specialized lab herself and was told that no information could be given to her directly. The results had to be sent back to the commercial laboratory, which would then send them to her provider, who would tell her of the findings. When she pointed out that one month had passed and time was running out if follow-up testing was needed, an exception was made to the lab's policy and she was told that the results were inconclusive.

It turns out that the laboratory did not analyze the right blood component. At the time of the test the lab was in disarray, without a laboratory director or a firm protocol. This is not a unique case.

Another laboratory on record has had repeated power failures. During these periods, all the amniotic fluid cells had to be discarded, and many women had to repeat these invasive procedures. Some women, by not being told why their tests needed to be repeated, were caused needless anxiety. One doctor told his client, "Your baby's cells did not grow, so we need to repeat the test."

Ask your health care provider if s/he knows the practices of the laboratory. Sometimes specimens for genetic studies are sent to a laboratory that transfers it to another laboratory, perhaps even one out of state. Your provider may or may not know this, and it could be important. Ask your provider which laboratory s/he uses, what are her experiences with the particular lab, and what is the lab's "track record."

Another important question to ask is whether or not the lab participates in a voluntary external quality-control program under which a certain number of prenatal samples are periodically sent to an outside reference laboratory, which processes the samples. The results are compared with those of the original lab for precision and accuracy. A laboratory that recognizes the importance of external quality control is likely to be one that cares about its performance.

INFORMED CONSENT/REFUSAL

Since most of us have little understanding of genetics, we generally look to our physician for enlightenment. This means that you should choose an obstetric provider who has reasonable knowledge about prenatal testing and who keeps abreast of the times.

You and your physician enter into a contractual relationship when s/he agrees to care for you and you agree to let the provider use her/his professional knowledge to guide you. This relationship is unlike the normal commercial arrangement of buyer and seller, where, if the buyer does not ask, the seller is under no duty to disclose risks. A physician has the duty to disclose all information about tests or treatments. Providing all the facts is the basis of "informed consent."

This concept has only recently entered our culture. It used to be that physicians did not disclose to their patients. Hippocrates advised doctors to perform their duties "adroitly and calmly, concealing most things from the patient." This was thought to be for the good of the patient. Of course, it also kept medical practice a mystery to all but the physician.

With prenatal testing, informed consent requires that you have an understanding of the procedures, goals, benefits, and risks prior to each test. At some point, you may be asked to sign an informed consent/refusal form. This form attests that you know about the test and have made your own decision to choose or refuse the test. The form then becomes a permanent part of your medical record. It also protects your physician from liability. Carefully review the informed consent form that is used by your provider before deciding upon prenatal testing. If s/he does not use a form, at least get a verbal version of such an agreement.

CONFIDENTIALITY OF GENETIC DATA

Genetic-related information should be private because it could significantly affect many areas of your life—your employment choices as well as your personal, financial, and psychological life.

The Federal Privacy Act of 1974 requires that well-formulated procedures be set up by states to protect the rights of privacy of individuals and their families. Confidentiality of medical records and personal communication is especially important. Policies maintaining privacy of communication and testing results, prohibiting storage of noncoded information in data banks, and limiting access only to anonymous data for statistical purposes are essential, but safeguards are rarely in place. In fact, agencies are constantly collecting data for use in developing policies on resource allocation, medical costs, and to identify conditions for future research. You may have no choice as to whether your test results are among those statistics collected or those that are "stolen" from computers.

Health and insurance companies sometimes use genetic information to exclude people from coverage. Employers may not hire people whose genetic profile may indicate potential illness.

As the availability of genetic information grows, pressures to use it or disclose it to third parties will increase unless protective legislation and safeguards are put into place. Before you have any genetic screening tests, inquire about the mechanisms available to assure that your results will remain confidential. Ask your provider if s/he is taking part in any data-collecting programs and if your anonymity will be protected.

WAITING FOR TEST RESULTS

If you're considering prenatal testing, you may as well recognize that the stresses of the situation do not cease after the test. For many women, waiting for results can seem like a lifetime. It's often hard to follow the medical advice to "relax and forget about it for a few weeks." Depending on how far along you are in your pregnancy, you may be feeling your baby move. At the same time, if you think you would have an abortion if a disability does exist, you may feel reluctant to develop any sort of connection to the fetus. As sociologist Barbara Katz-Rothman writes, "Women wait in this limbo of 'tentative pregnancy' unsure of whether they are 'mothers' or carriers of a disabled fetus." The waiting time will make demands on you and you should be prepared to take care of yourself.

THE RESULTS

If you are considering prenatal testing, there are several outcomes you should be prepared for. You may be told that "everything is fine." Your obstetric provider may say "something seems to be wrong." (See chapter 4.)

But you may also get a result that says a test is "uninformative."

This means that there is not sufficient information on which to make a diagnosis or interpretation about the health of your fetus. You may have to repeat the test or have another type of test. It may be that other family members will need to undergo testing.

A *negative* prenatal test means that the test is *normal.* Although the word "negative" connotes to most of us something bad, with prenatal tests, a negative result usually means that further testing is not indicated.

A *positive* test means that the test result is *abnormal.* In some instances further testing can be done to look for the cause of this finding or to confirm it.

The way in which you will be told about your results will vary. You may receive test results in the form of a letter. If a specialist has performed the test, the letter may come from the specialist, or the results may be communicated to you by your primary health care provider.

There really is no satisfactory approach for a midwife, doctor, or counselor to tell a woman her baby may be disabled, but some health care providers are better at this than others. There are reports of really inept handling of this delicate matter. For example, women have been called at home late Friday night and told, "Things don't look good. Make an appointment to come in next week." Or the partner has been given the news over the phone and then made responsible for telling the pregnant woman.

If you choose prenatal testing, talk with your provider about the approach s/he will take in giving you the results. In some practices, the nurse or counselor will call if results are normal, and the doctor will call if they are abnormal. You can probably work out something like this so you will know what to expect. You may want to request that your provider give you written material and tell you about support resources if s/he learns a disability may exist.

HOW TO PROCEED

1) First study the material on the individual tests. 2) Then read chapters 9 and 10 for evaluating how you will deal with these tests. 3) Chapters 11 through 15 show you how to make the deci-

sions for yourself based on your genetic/environmental profile and your own needs. All three of these things—the specific tests, your own profile, and the consequences of the test results—must play a part in your decision to have or refuse each prenatal test.

Deciding on prenatal testing is a large responsibility. It's an important decision—for you and your baby.

BOOK TWO

The Tests

4

Maternal Serum Alpha-Fetoprotein (MSAFP) Screening Test

The most common—and controversial—test that you may be offered during pregnancy is maternal serum alpha-fetoprotein (MSAFP) screening, a genetic screening test that is used to identify the few women whose fetuses may be at risk for certain disabilities.

WHAT IS A MSAFP SCREENING TEST?

MSAFP is a blood test that measures the amount of alpha-fetoprotein (AFP) in your blood. AFP is a substance that occurs naturally during pregnancy. It is produced by the fetus and is excreted in the fetal urine, which composes the amniotic fluid. AFP then passes from the amniotic fluid through the placenta and into a woman's bloodstream, where it can be measured.

The amount of AFP in the blood at certain stages of pregnancy has been associated with genetic variations in the fetus. The results generated by the MSAFP screening test can only help you decide whether or not to have further diagnostic tests, like ultrasound and amniocentesis. By itself it does not yield definitive results.

USES OF MSAFP SCREENING

The MSAFP screening test has been estimated to identify 80 percent to 90 percent of open neural tube conditions such as spina bifida (p. 223) and anencephaly (p. 222) in the fetus and approximately 20 percent of unborn babies with Down syndrome (p. 211). In other words, there is a 10 percent to 20 percent chance that a fetus with an open neural tube disorder will not be identified and an 80 percent chance that a fetus with Down syndrome will not be detected. This test identifies some, but not all, women who have a higher likelihood of carrying a fetus with one of these conditions. Other rare conditions such as gastrochisis (an opening in the abdominal wall) might also be identified.

   MSAFP screening is beginning to be used for later pregnancy management. Some researchers theorize that the MSAFP screening test could be used to predict which babies will experience stress in the last trimester and those that might be born prematurely or with low birth weight, weighing less than five and a half pounds.

MSAFP SCREENING FOR WHOM?

At the present time, the American College of Obstetricians and Gynecologists recommends that physicians offer MSAFP screening to all pregnant women. In many states this recommendation has translated into the medical practice of performing MSAFP screening on all pregnant women with or without their consent.

TIMING THE MSAFP TEST

If you choose to have the MSAFP screening test, it should be performed sixteen to eighteen weeks after the first day of your last menstrual period (LMP). The test must be done at the proper time to ensure accurate results. Try to schedule this test for the fifteenth or sixteenth week to allow adequate time in your pregnancy for decision-making about diagnostic follow-up tests if the MSAFP test results are abnormal.

Choose a provider who will be able to link you up immediately with follow-up services if they are necessary. It is also helpful if the laboratory doing this test is equipped to do follow-up studies. In general, laboratories connected with universities are more likely to make recommendations and provide follow-up services than are most of the commercial labs.

COSTS OF MSAFP SCREENING

The cost for the MSAFP screening test varies among laboratories analyzing the blood, although the price range usually is between thirty-five dollars and fifty dollars. At this time most insurance companies do not cover the cost of this screening test.

INFORMED CONSENT

Some providers will do the test routinely without asking your permission, while others will require that you sign an informed consent form.

THE MSAFP SCREENING PROCEDURE

Performing the MSAFP blood test is relatively easy. During one of your prenatal visits between the sixteenth to eighteenth week, your health care provider will take a sample of blood from your arm. This will be sent to a laboratory that will analyze it to determine the quantity of AFP it contains.

RECEIVING MSAFP RESULTS

A laboratory usually knows the results of the MSAFP screening test within a few days, but results are often not released until weeks after the blood sample is received. Each lab designates certain days of the week to "run the test." For example, some labs only perform the test on Tuesday mornings. If your blood arrives at the lab late Tuesday afternoon, it might be stored until the next batch is analyzed the following week. Your results will not be known until the next cycle is completed, and by the time your health care provider and you receive results, one to two weeks may have passed.

Ask your provider how each of you will be notified about the result. Usually, you will receive a letter that will inform you of your test result. (See p. 51 for how results are calculated.)

If your result is abnormal, the letter may suggest that you call your provider for discussion and information regarding follow-up tests. Some laboratories would delay sending you notification of abnormal results for several days to allow time for your health care provider to call you first. In the interests of time, the lab should inform your provider by telephone of all abnormal test results. If you are worried about the test, you can request that you be contacted immediately whether the result is normal or abnormal.

NORMAL MSAFP RESULTS

Approximately 950 out of every 1,000 pregnant women who are screened show a normal MSAFP test result. Even though they are carrying a healthy baby, 48 to 49 out of every 1,000 women will have elevated results and a few will have low results. Only one or two women of every 1,000 women screened will actually have a fetus with a disability. To put it another way, an MSAFP result in the normal range cannot guarantee a normal baby at birth—as no prenatal test will. Nor, as the figures show, will an abnormal result necessarily mean that your baby has a disability.

ELEVATED MSAFP TEST RESULTS

Several factors can cause an elevated result. For example, if you are further along in your pregnancy than you originally thought—even if your dates are off by only one week—this miscalculation can change your results. Unsuspected twins can cause an elevated MSAFP level because, even though each fetus is producing a normal amount of AFP, it can look like a higher than normal level from one fetus. Current research also suggests that MSAFP levels may be slightly elevated if the fetus is male.

If the result of your first blood sample is high, do not consider this result final. Depending on the elevation, your health care provider will either obtain a new blood sample and repeat the test immediately or will suggest an ultrasound test. In most instances, the results of the repeat test will be in the normal range and further testing will not be indicated. If the repeat test shows an elevated level of AFP, ultrasound testing can be done to look for the possible cause. For example, you might be carrying twins, or your dates may be off. If the ultrasound test explains the elevated test results, no further testing will be indicated. If it does not, amniocentesis will be suggested.

LOW MSAFP TEST RESULTS

The most common cause of a low MSAFP level is that you are not as far along in your pregnancy as you thought. If your calculation of dates is off by even one week, the test can be interpreted falsely as abnormal. Researchers also say that slightly low MSAFP levels occur when the fetus is female.

Abnormally low levels of AFP may also occur if you have maternal insulin-dependent diabetes mellitus, or in the presence of chromosome anomalies, or because of a false (molar) pregnancy.

Recent research has found an association between low levels of AFP and the presence of Down syndrome, but further research is necessary to determine the significance of this relationship. In 1984, researchers conducted a retrospective study to look at infants born to women who had low levels of AFP in their blood during pregnancy. They noticed that women with low MSAFP levels had a higher-than-usual incidence of having a baby with Down syndrome. Their research suggests that a fetus with Down syndrome produces, for some unknown reason, less AFP than normal. Although this association is still under study, many countries already use the MSAFP test for Down syndrome screening and have integrated it into their routine obstetrical practice.

If the results of your first MSAFP screening test show a low level of AFP, again, do not consider the results final. The results must be tabulated along with your age, race, weight, and week of pregnancy. Then, using a mathematical chart, your doctor should be able to calculate a more accurate "risk figure" for Down syndrome. This process generally produces more reliable risk figures than a formula calculated on age alone.

If the "new" calculated risk figure is still low, your provider may suggest an ultrasound test. If ultrasound does not explain the low AFP value, amniocentesis to study fetal chromosomes may be recommended.

It is not the practice to retest a low blood sample. AFP normally increases as pregnancy progresses and, in theory, the second test may move toward normal and might give false reassurance that the baby does not have Down syndrome when in fact it may. On the other hand, when the first result is elevated, or high, the repeat test will generally be within normal limits if a neural tube condition is not present or your dates were off. When twins or spina bifida exists, the repeat test will continue to show elevated levels of AFP.

CAUSES OF ELEVATED MSAFP LEVELS

- Your pregnancy is further along than you thought.

- You are carrying twins.

- There may have been bleeding at or near your placenta at some time during your pregnancy.

- You may have a medical condition (such as liver disease) that is affecting the test results.

- The fetus has a neural tube disorder or a rare stomach or intestinal condition.

CAUSES OF LOW MSAFP LEVELS

• Your pregnancy is less advanced than you originally thought.

• You may have a medical condition (such as diabetes) that is affecting the test results.

• This is a "false pregnancy."

• The fetus has Down syndrome.

CALCULATING RESULTS

Your results will be reported in a number that gives the risk rate of a disorder occurring in your pregnancy. This is expressed as an MoM, a Multiple of the Median—really a measure of your result relative to others. This is a relative figure and must be adjusted for your personal profile.

To understand the mathematics involved in calculating the MSAFP test results, look at Table 1. This table illustrates how the risk of Down syndrome is influenced by a woman's age and her MSAFP level. (This particular table is used by the Foundation for Blood Research in Scarborough, Maine, one of the country's leading external quality-control programs for MSAFP screening.) Although this table should not be used to determine your personal risk estimate, it can give you an idea of what numbers and risk rates have been generated.

Note that these figures are based on the occurrence of Down syndrome at fifteen to twenty weeks of pregnancy. These risk rates are much higher than what would be expected at birth, since many fetuses with an abnormality will be miscarried. For example, a woman thirty-two years old who is fifteen to twenty weeks pregnant is said to have a 1-in-560 chance that she is carrying a fetus with Down syndrome. If she has the MSAFP screening test and it is 0.5 MoM, her chances may increase to 1 in 240. On the other hand, if her MSAFP reading is 1.2 MoM, her chances decrease to 1 in 980.

Table 1
ODDS OF DOWN SYNDROME AT
15–20 WEEKS GESTATION
(NOT AT DELIVERY)

Maternal Age	Odds Based On Age Alone	Risk if MSAFP 0.5 MoM	Risk if MSAFP 1.5 MoM
20	1/1230	1:600	1:2900
22	1/1070	1:520	1:2500
24	1/940	1:470	1:2300
26	1/840	1:420	1:2000
28	1/760	1:370	1:1800
30	1/690	1:330	1:1580
32	1/560	1:260	1:1270
34	1/350	1:159	1:770
35	1/270	1:115	1:148
36	1/210	1:94	1:460
38	1/129	1:57	1:280
40	1/78	1:33	1:135

This table is created from data as presented by Palomaki et al. in "Maternal Serum Gynecol," 1987; 156:460-3.

"Alpha-fetoprotein, Age and Down Syndrome Risk" in Am J Obstet

ACCURACY OF MSAFP TEST

The MSAFP screening test is thought to be 90 percent accurate as a screening test for neural tube disorders. However, it can produce false positive and false negative results and interpretations.

"False positive" is a result or interpretation that incorrectly indicates the presence of a disease or condition. For example, a false positive result suggests that a fetus has a neural tube disorder when, in fact, it does not.

"False negative" is a result or interpretation that incorrectly indicates the absence of a disease or condition. For example, a false negative test can incorrectly suggest that a fetus does not have a neural tube disorder when, in fact, the fetus does have one. A false negative interpretation in the detection of neural tube conditions is rare. However, a false negative interpretation in the detection of Down syndrome is quite common. (Preliminary data suggest that the test can only identify 20 percent of all fetuses screened for Down syndrome.)

These inaccuracies happen for a variety of reasons, some of which are listed here:

• If the person performing the test is inexperienced. For example, if too little blood is collected, the test cannot be processed. This makes a repeat test necessary—and may delay the test until it is too late to be accurate.

• If the test kit itself has been sitting on the shelf too long, the active ingredients and chemicals in it may have expired.

• If the laboratory has not generated its own reference values or calculated its own range of normal limits for the population being screened. In this case the conclusions it reaches may not be accurate.

• If the laboratory gives your health care provider only the numerical values with reference data and expects her/him to interpret the test. This occurs most often in commercial laboratories that do not employ a medical doctor to make interpretations. If your provider uses such a commercial lab, is s/he familiar enough with the test to make an accurate interpretation? Before consenting to the procedure ask your provider which type of laboratory your blood specimen will be sent to and who will do the interpretation.

• If the personal-profile information accompanying your blood sample is insufficient. Factors such as your age, race, weight, general medical condition, the gestational age of the fetus, and the date and time the sample was drawn, must be included along with the blood sample for an accurate interpretation. Not including this information is the most frequent problem in interpreting the results of this test.

Discuss with your health care provider ways to prevent these common problems from occurring. They are not trivial concerns.

As a result of errors and misjudgments in connection with this early test, many women are subjected to unnecessary ultrasound and amniocentesis—tests that are far more complicated than the MSAFP. Therefore, if you have the MSAFP test, monitor it carefully. You may be making major life decisions based on its results.

This almost happened in the case of one woman who had the MSAFP screening test. She received a report that her MSAFP level was elevated, putting her at 2.4 MoM. This figure was plotted on a curve, taking into account her weight and how far along she thought she was in her pregnancy. This value was interpreted as high for 16.8 weeks gestation.

The woman decided to repeat the test and at the same time conduct a small experiment. She sent three blood samples to three different laboratories. The laboratory she originally used returned a report of 1.7 MoM. They interpreted this as normal for 17 weeks and suggested no further testing.

The second lab reported a MSAFP value of 1.2 MoM. Although the numbers differed from the first laboratory, they, too, were interpreted as normal for 17.3 weeks gestation and again no further testing was indicated.

The third lab reported a value of 2.1 MoM. According to them, the level of MSAFP was elevated for 16.9 weeks of pregnancy. They recommended that an ultrasound test be done immediately to confirm the timing of the pregnancy and to rule out any apparent fetal disabilities. They also recommended amniocentesis if there was any suspicion of a problem.

The third lab had based its calculations on a different gestational age than the other two had. Rather than rounding up her dates from 16.9 to 17 weeks gestation, the lab used a formula for 16 weeks. If the protocol of the third lab based its calculations on 17 weeks of pregnancy, the results would have been 1.8 MoM—or "normal."

The accuracy of this test depends on how it is done, who is directing the laboratory, what protocol has been established, and what hidden agenda, if any, exists. If, for example, the third laboratory favored the use of prenatal testing, their protocol might have a narrower range of normal. They might therefore consider more blood samples "abnormal" and require follow-up testing.

RISKS

Aside from the usual risk of having a blood sample taken and the emotional stress that may be entailed, there are no risks to the woman or the fetus from taking this test.

THE MSAFP CONTROVERSY

This test serves as an example of what happens when new technologies come to the marketplace too soon. Until recently, the MSAFP screening test was restricted to use in research-type settings where test performance was carefully monitored and follow-up programs were in place. But in 1984 the Federal Drug Administration (FDA) concluded that restrictions on the sale and distribution of the MSAFP test were not necessary. This meant that any manufacturer could make the product and any laboratory could perform the MSAFP test and determine results.

Since that decision, AFP anxiety has increased. In addition, experience worldwide has shown that there are problems with the quality of the test itself. Numerous companies have developed products that vary in safety and accuracy. Another problem is that some tests/products are being used to screen for disabilities they were not developed to study. This greatly affects their accuracy.

The New England Journal of Medicine has become a forum for ongoing debate about the quality of the individual test kits. Articles cite certain manufacturers for producing relatively good test kits, and question the kits produced by others.

Another aspect of the MSAFP controversy concerns the issue of obstetric liability. In the last few years, health care providers have seen their insurance costs rise at alarming rates. As a result, they often suggest tests that would seem to reduce the range of unknown variables. The major consequence of this practice of defensive medicine is that it generates unnecessary worry and concern about the health of our unborn children.

At this time, the MSAFP screening test is voluntary and requires informed decision-making. However, some states are hoping to mandate MSAFP screening of all pregnant women. Unless we begin to discuss and debate the benefits of this prenatal screening test soon, we may have no choice.

As you can see, the MSAFP screening test requires careful thinking before you enter the complicated testing process. It requires skilled health professionals who understand the details of the entire screening process and can help guide your decisions.

You now know what the MSAFP process is. Before you choose to have or decline the procedure, read Book Three (p. 149), "To Test or Not to Test."

The following self-awareness exercise is meant only to help you clarify for yourself why you are considering this test.

The Choice for MSAFP Screening

A. Check your reasons for considering the MSAFP screening test.

- ☐ My doctor wants me to have it.

- ☐ It's part of the prenatal package.

- ☐ It may signal that there is a problem with the health of my baby.

- ☐ It may suggest whether I should consider further testing such as ultrasound or amniocentesis.

- ☐ I don't want to feel guilty that I did not take advantage of the technology.

- ☐ Other pregnant women are having it.

B. Write down any other reasons. _____

_____

_____

_____

The Choice Against MSAFP Screening

A. Check your reasons for NOT wanting the MSAFP screening test.

☐ I don't want unnecessary testing.

☐ It's just a screening test and is not very accurate.

☐ There is too much variability in the way each laboratory processes it.

☐ I feel that it's just the beginning of more testing.

☐ I am afraid of what I might find out.

☐ It's not covered by insurance.

B. Write down any other reasons. _____

_____

_____

_____

Now that you have clarified your own thinking about MSAFP screening, discuss it with your partner and your health care provider. Then consult Book Three (p. 149) for help in choosing or refusing this test.

5 | Ultrasound

The day has arrived when ultrasound in pregnancy is routine. Many women have at least one ultrasound during pregnancy, and some two or three, despite the fact that the risks to future generations have not been fully assessed and questions about long-term safety remain unanswered. Most women do not realize that fetal ultrasound is still an "experimental" procedure.

WHAT IS ULTRASOUND?

Fetal ultrasound, known as obstetric or diagnostic ultrasound, ultrasonography, or a sonogram, has become a window to the womb. Used to examine the fetus inside the uterus, it is the only noninvasive (nonsurgical) technique that allows us to visualize the fetus *in utero*. It is used for many reasons, including to detect certain fetal disabilities and to determine whether further prenatal tests should be considered.

Ultrasound is composed of sound waves that are converted to electrical energy to reflect a black-and-white picture on a televisionlike screen. Bone shows up as white, while tissue looks black. Ultrasound produces two physical effects on tissue that enables a picture to be made—heat, and a process called "cavitation" in which bubbles are created in response to the sound waves. At extremely high energy levels, fetal tissues can heat up and the amniotic fluid can bubble.

Ultrasound is actually a form of radiation (it is nonionizing versus ionizing radiation that is emitted by X ray). A medical journal recently stated that the term *ultrasound radiation* "may confuse nonexperts in the field," and therefore ultrasound is not usually referred to by its full name.

THE EQUIPMENT USED IN ULTRASOUND

There are several different types of ultrasound equipment used during pregnancy. Each one records information in a different way, but they all work on the same principle—the use of sound waves to create an image.

Level One examinations, the simplest method of ultrasound, are used to create one- or two-dimensional pictures. These are used to document baseline data such as fetal age, size, weight, presentation, placental location, and appearance of major fetal body parts.

Real time ultrasound: Real time ultrasound, used for a Level Two examination, is the most sophisticated type of ultrasonography. It combines still pictures in rapid succession to show movement similar to the frames of a motion picture. This type of ultrasound shows the movements of the fetus—the fetal heartbeat, breathing, arm and leg motions, and functions such as swallowing. It is used alone for prenatal diagnosis or in conjunction with amniocentesis, chorionic villus sampling, or fetal blood sampling.

Doppler ultrasound: Doppler ultrasound is used to evaluate fetal heart rate. One type is a hand-held device frequently used during prenatal care visits to listen to fetal heart sounds. Doppler ultrasound is actually thought to emit more sound-wave exposure than the types of ultrasound described above because it emits a continuous wave beam rather than an intermittent one. Doppler ultrasound is also used late in pregnancy when a woman is considered "overdue," when the estimated birth date has passed. In a healthy fetus the heart rate will change and return to normal during the contractions of pregnancy. If the rate does not change and readjust, the fetus is considered to be "in distress." Because it measures fetal heart rate, ultrasound is used to screen for fetal distress. Very little is known about the effects of this exposure, yet because Doppler ultrasound is within economic reach of most physicians, it is in wide use.

If ultrasound is used only to monitor the baby's heart and if you are concerned about ultrasound exposure, request that your health care provider listen to the fetal heart with a fetoscope, an instrument similar to a stethoscope.

Developments in ultrasonography equipment include high resolution, automation, and computer analysis, even machines to generate colored pictures. New applications of ultrasound are being proposed, such as umbilical artery Doppler ultrasound. Neither their accuracy nor their risk has yet been evaluated.

USES OF ULTRASOUND

In the hands of an experienced operator, ultrasound can be used to identify some structural variations of the head, spine, heart, lungs, arms, legs, fingers, toes, kidneys, bladder, bowels, and abdomen.

Recent attention has also been given to the use of ultrasound in the detection of Down syndrome. According to certain studies, ultrasound identifies a fetus with Down syndrome by revealing a characteristic extra skin fold on the back of the neck. Although amniocentesis is the procedure that most accurately diagnoses Down syndrome, ultrasound may soon be used as a screening test for this condition.

Ultrasound as an Adjunct to Prenatal Diagnosis
Ultrasound is used to guide instruments during prenatal procedures like amniocentesis, chorionic villus sampling, and percutaneous umbilical blood sampling. It allows the doctor to see where the fetus, placenta, and umbilical cord are located, in order to avoid injury during the needle insertion. Ultrasound should always be used continuously during these procedures.

OTHER USES OF ULTRASOUND

If you are considering ultrasound, be sure that you know the purpose of the information you'll receive and what steps can then be taken to improve your health or that of your unborn baby. Ultrasound may be offered to you for the following reasons:

To Confirm Your Pregnancy

You and/or your doctor may want an ultrasound "to confirm your pregnancy." By the fifth week of pregnancy the amniotic sac and the fetus can be detected, and limb movements are often apparent at nine weeks.

However, consider carefully whether you want to have an ultrasound for this purpose. Perhaps you would rather just observe the changes in your body (like a missed period, breast tenderness, frequency of urination, and enlargement of your uterus) to assure yourself that you're pregnant, rather than letting technology confirm it for you. You could also have the blood test human chorionic gonadotropin (HCG) or use an at-home pregnancy test kit if you are too curious to wait for nature's signs.

To See the Location of Your Baby

Some doctors use ultrasound to look for the location or presentation of the baby. It is also used to rule out an ectopic pregnancy (one that implants outside rather than inside the uterus).

To Figure Out Your Baby's Age (Pregnancy Dating)

Your doctor may consider it important to know your baby's age if (1) you are uncertain of the first date of your last menstrual period; (2) if your MSAFP level is abnormal; or (3) if you have a condition that makes you "high risk."

Pregnancy dating by ultrasound is most accurate during the first half of pregnancy. Even in the hands of an expert, however, ultrasound can only give an estimate of fetal age. One method of dating involves measuring the sac at five to seven weeks. This is accurate plus or minus ten days. After seven weeks the sac might be distorted by the bladder and changes in the uterus. A measurement of the baby from head to bottom (crown-rump length) can be obtained between the seventh and fourteenth week. At six to seven weeks the accuracy is plus or minus three days.

Measurements are not as accurate after the fourteenth week. At this time the curvature of the fetal spine changes, the fetus may be longer than the length of the ultrasound screen, and fetal motion interferes with obtaining this type of measurement. After the fourteenth week the biparietal diameter (BPD) of the baby's head, the femur length, and head and abdominal circumferences are used to estimate age. Between 14 and 26 weeks the accuracy of these measurements is plus or minus seven to ten days. Between twenty-nine and forty weeks the accuracy may be plus or minus twenty-one days. Performing what's called a "biophysical profile," which includes monitoring the fetal heart rate by stress testing, and observing fetal activity by real time ultrasound, is also common in the third trimester of pregnancy if a woman is thought to be "overdue."

Many women in early pregnancy classes ask, "Isn't it important to know exactly when I am due?" The answer is, "Not if the person taking care of you promises to be at your delivery no matter when it occurs." If your dates are "off" or a reason for a discrepancy is found, ask your health care provider beforehand what you will be able to do with the information. Are there further tests or therapies? Will it mean a series of further ultrasounds to observe any changes? How will this information help you?

To See If There Is More than One Baby

In the past, the birth of twins was often a surprise, both to the mother and the doctor. Often, though, during a physical examination, a skilled clinician could feel more than one fetus and hear two hearts beat as the pregnancy progressed. Today a physician's diagnosis can be confirmed. Now there are many doctors who put their hands on a woman's belly and say, "Hmm, you may have two little ones in there. Why don't we do an ultrasound just to see?"

Although ultrasound can show whether or not you are carrying more than one baby, it is not necessary to determine this special condition. Carefully consider whether you want ultrasound to see if you are carrying more than one fetus. Being pregnant with twins may put a pregnancy at higher risk for growth and placental problems or premature labor. Some doctors might perform a series of ultrasounds up until the end of pregnancy. Other doctors and midwives do not see the need to do even one. Some doctors like to use an ultrasound to see the position and presentation of the twins when deciding upon a cesarean section or vaginal birth. Some doctors will do a cesarean section whenever more than one baby is present. Others will deliver twins vaginally and even at home.

To Check Your Baby's Growth

Your health care provider may recommend ultrasound if the age of your unborn baby and the expected size of your uterus do not correlate. If your provider feels that you look "too small" or "too big" for your stage of pregnancy, s/he may want to look inside to see if there is a reason. But the definitions of small-for-gestational and large-for-gestational age are statistical and therefore are arbitrary methods for growth evaluation. Although there are estimates of where your fetus should be in relation to your uterus, babies grow at a different pace and nestle into the pelvic structure differently. Many of the standards for determining a "normal growth range" were actually generated years ago when nutritional advice and recommendations for weight gain were very different from what they are now. It wasn't too long ago, for example, that women were told to gain no more than eighteen pounds during pregnancy. Now the recommendation is at least twenty-five pounds.

Rare conditions like fetal growth retardation, or intrauterine growth retardation (IUGR) that can be caused by viral infections, smoking, alcoholism, drugs, or poor perfusion of nutrients from the placenta to the fetus can often be diagnosed by ultrasound. Assessing fetal weight may also be useful in a situation where there is premature rupture of the membranes or premature labor begins.

Once again, consider carefully whether you want an ultrasound to check your baby's growth. If you learn that there is a growth-related condition, ask your health care provider what you can do with the information.

To Evaluate Movement, Tone, and Breathing

As part of a general assessment of the fetus, some doctors perform an ultrasound to evaluate movement, muscle tone, and breathing. Actual movements of the baby's chest wall can be seen by eleven weeks of pregnancy and breathing has been noted by the sixteenth week. But keep in mind that women have reliably experienced fetal movement or "quickening" between the seventeenth and twentieth week of pregnancy. Your perception of your baby's activity may be a reliable enough measure of his/her movement and tone.

To Identify the Baby's Sex

Some women have an ultrasound to find out if they are carrying a girl or a boy. Although ultrasound is used to identify a baby's sex, it is not recommended for this purpose, nor is it always accurate. Basically, your doctor will try to look between your baby's legs and make a guess about the sex. Sometimes the umbilical cord is between the legs so the genitals can't be seen. Amniocentesis is more accurate for this purpose though not recommended to determine sex alone. (See p. 75.)

Carefully consider whether you want to know the sex of your fetus or if you want to be surprised. Prior to an ultrasound for any purpose, let your doctor know whether or not you want to be told if you are carrying a boy or a girl.

To Assess the Amount of Amniotic Fluid

There is thought to be a correlation between the amount of amniotic fluid at different points in pregnancy and fetal health. However, estimates of the amount of amniotic fluid volume are subjective because they are made by simply looking at the screen, and at any given time there will be some variation in the amount of amniotic fluid.

In rare instances, too much or too little amniotic fluid may indicate a variety of conditions. Too much fluid may be associated with twins, diabetes mellitus, Rh incompatibility, or a disability such as hydrocephalus, "water on the brain." Too little fluid may occur if the baby has a growth problem or a urinary tract alteration.

As an Adjunct to Cervical Cerclage
Ultrasound may be used to place a cervical cerclage, or suture, in women who have had premature opening of the cervix in pregnancy called "cervical incompetence" by obstetricians. Ultrasound is used to time the placement and removal of the suture and to assure its position.

To Look for Molar Pregnancies
Ultrasound imaging can be useful if a pregnancy seems to be progressing, but a heartbeat cannot be detected by the fourteenth week. There are a few growths (such as a hydatidiform mole, cysts, or tumors) that can mimic a pregnancy in that they elevate blood hormone levels and cause the uterus to enlarge.

To Determine the Structure and Position of the Placenta
The health of the placenta—the lifeline—influences the health of the baby. Ultrasound can identify structural or positional variations, as well as determine the size and maturity of the placenta. Ultrasound can also determine the position of the placenta relative to the opening of the cervix, but it is accurate for this purpose only in the third trimester. Approximately 50 percent of placentas are low in the first and second trimesters of pregnancy and might be falsely regarded as "placenta previa," a placenta that may partially cover the cervix. Some physicians cause inappropriate concern in early pregnancy by telling the woman she may need to deliver by cesarean section because of this low placenta. A decision about a cesarean section should not be based on a first or second trimester ultrasound report of a low placenta. Ultrasound, however, is often used in later pregnancy for women who have previously had placenta previa.

Ultrasound is also used to assess the structural health of the placenta. Changes can be observed in the presence of maternal and fetal conditions, such as chronic high blood pressure, maternal diabetes, and Rh disease. Changes on the surface of the placenta, such as extra lobes, tumors, or scarring, can also be seen.

For Causes of Bleeding

Vaginal spotting in early pregnancy is not uncommon. The new blood vessels that are forming may be fragile or sensitive. Spotting can occur when the embryo is embedding into the uterus or around the time that your first period is due. Some health care providers will suggest an ultrasound if spotting has occurred. Others will suggest you rest until the spotting stops.

Heavy bleeding may indicate an increased chance of a miscarriage in the first trimester. Ultrasound may be able to identify the source of bleeding and the status of the fetus. It can help determine whether bleeding is caused by premature separation of the placenta (placental abruption) and whether hospitalization might be needed.

During Fetal Surgery

Ultrasound visualization and assessment of the fetus have resulted in the diagnosis of a number of disabilities, some of which may be amenable to treatment *in utero*. Fetal surgery, still an experimental technique, is being used in conjunction with ultrasound for conditions such as urinary-tract obstructions, hydrocephalus, and intravascular blood transfusions.

To Confirm Fetal Death

The absence of fetal movement is a sign of fetal distress or death. Real time ultrasound scanning can diagnose fetal death by documenting lack of a fetal heartbeat. If you suspect that your fetus has died, you can decide whether or not you want ultrasound to confirm this finding, or whether you would rather wait and let your body deal with it naturally via miscarriage. If the time between fetal demise and expulsion becomes prolonged, a D&C abortion may be suggested in order to remove any remaining fetal contents and to prevent complications.

THE TIMING FOR ULTRASOUND

Ultrasound is used throughout pregnancy for a variety of purposes, most of which involve enabling physicians to have a better grasp of the pregnancy. But if you are considering ultrasound to screen for disabilities in your unborn baby, it should be performed between the sixteenth and eighteenth week of pregnancy. By the sixteenth week the major fetal body parts are formed. In the rare instance that a structural problem exists, you will have time to think about your options, including possible follow-up diagnostic tests.

COSTS OF ULTRASOUND

The cost of ultrasound varies between $150 and $300. Not all insurance companies and Medicaid programs cover the cost of this procedure. Still, no woman should be denied an ultrasound because of an inability to pay. Get in touch with your local state genetics program (appendix pp. 246–251) to find out how you can get financial assistance.

INFORMED CONSENT

Ultrasound is often given automatically without even verbal consent. Although informed consent is not applied to Doppler or other modes of ultrasound, the procedure should not be treated lightly and should include the use of an informed consent form that documents the type of ultrasound, its length, and exposure.

PREPARATION FOR ULTRASOUND

If you are going to have an ultrasound, you may be asked to drink several glasses of fluid a few hours before the procedure is scheduled. You will also be told not to urinate until the ultrasound procedure is over. Your full bladder serves as a landmark during the ultrasound procedure. It helps the ultrasonographer locate your pelvic organs and it makes your uterus more visible.

THE ULTRASOUND PROCEDURE

For an ultrasound examination, you will be asked to lie on a narrow table and to expose your abdomen from the lower part of

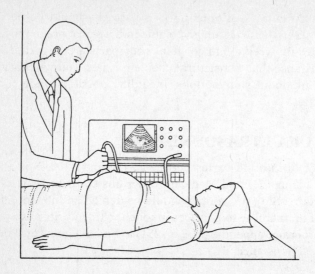

your ribs to your hips. Wear a shirt and slacks for this procedure, rather than skirt or dress. Some cold mineral oil or gel will be put on your skin. The lights in the room are usually turned off at this point. A hand-held device called a transducer will be placed on your abdomen and will be moved around it to scan the area.

The transducer will now begin to transmit ultrasound waves through the body. As these waves pass through your uterus, they will encounter different densities and reflect back toward the transducer, like an echo. The returned sound waves are converted into electrical energy by the ultrasound equipment, and a black-and-white image of your baby will be reflected on a screen. Depending on the reason for your ultrasound, your health care provider will take a series of measurements and will carefully examine all of the fetal parts. Many ultrasound machines have camera equipment attached, which allows still photos to be taken. Depending on the purpose of the test, the procedure takes anywhere from five to thirty minutes.

RECEIVING RESULTS

You will probably receive preliminary results during the actual procedure, but sometimes when an ultrasound technician performs the test, the results are given to your health care provider, who evaluates the exam and discusses the findings with you—probably by telephone. If you have been referred to another provider for the ultrasound, ask that a letter confirming the findings be sent to your doctor or midwife.

If you choose to have ultrasound to examine your developing baby, consider in advance how you want to handle any of the findings. Do you want to know about those situations in which findings may be of uncertain significance or where the condition may be transient? Some physicians withhold ambiguous information, believing that they are the filter for findings that are merely suspicions. Do you want to know if there is an abnormality as the ultrasound is occurring? If so, ask your doctor beforehand to share any suspicions during the actual scanning. If some sort of disability is present, it can be pointed out on the screen by the doctor while the testing is being done. If you don't want to know about any suspected variations at that time, tell your doctor in advance. One woman said, "I knew there was a problem. I could sense it. My doctor's glances and evasive answers were making me really anxious. I wanted to know what was happening and I felt relieved when he told me the truth."

FURTHER TESTING

Before making a major decision based on an "abnormal" ultrasound result, ask for a clear explanation of the possibility of diagnostic tests to confirm the results. For certain suspected conditions, amniocentesis or fetal blood sampling may be used as a follow-up, but, prior to exposing yourself to those tests, you may also want to seek a second opinion from a doctor who specializes in ultrasound.

ACCURACY OF ULTRASOUND

Ultrasound cannot diagnose all birth defects, and it can miss certain existing disabilities. False positive and false negative results and interpretations do occur. And obviously the accuracy of the test depends on the skill and experience of the person conducting the examination. For example, one woman who had an ultrasound was told that her fetus had spina bifida. Based on this assessment she arranged to have an abortion at a major teaching hospital. Before the abortion, the gynecologist sent her for another ultrasound to confirm her dates and to gather more information on the position of the fetus *in utero*. During the pre-abortion ultrasound the woman asked the technician, "How does it look?" And he, not realizing this was a pre-abortion ultrasound, said "Everything looks fine." Other professionals were called in immediately and all agreed that there was nothing wrong. The woman carried her pregnancy to term and went on to have a healthy baby at birth.

RISKS

How safe is ultrasound? A growing number of physicians and consumers are concerned about ultrasound exposure during pregnancy. According to many experts it is impossible to say that "diagnostic ultrasound is not harmful to the conceptus" or to call it safe. Many people are asking just what the criteria for "safe" actually are. Some doctors say the risk of ultrasound is largely theoretical, but others call ultrasound quack medicine.

To begin with what women experience, many doctors maintain that there is no discomfort during an ultrasound procedure. It's described as feeling like a "little tickle on your belly." However, some women have a different perception: One woman said, "I found it really uncomfortable to have a full bladder. On top of that I had to wait an extra hour because of a scheduling problem. Once I finally got settled the technician came in and pressed this transducer on my belly. My baby started going crazy, kicking and moving around. There I was lying flat on my back with a full bladder, my baby pushing at my rectum, and having this machine going around in circles on my abdomen. I couldn't wait for it to be over."

Ultrasound is receiving so much attention that recently a Consensus Development Conference of the National Institutes of Health (NIH) was convened to consider the use of ultrasound in pregnancy. The panel concluded that ultrasound could be useful in pregnancy but it shouldn't be used routinely. There was a lack of data and epidemiologic studies on ultrasound risk to the fetus. However, in reviewing animal-research studies using ultrasound, the panel revealed that altered growth, low birth weight, diminished immune response, changes in genetic material, cell death, teratogenic effects, and reduced reproductive potential did occur with high doses of ultrasound exposure. They concluded that in order to determine the long-term effects, the medical history of those children exposed prenatally to ultrasound should be followed for ten to fifteen years. In the final consensus statement, the NIH panel stated that more research on humans was needed.

Currently, no agency monitors exposure to ultrasound, and there has been little attempt to obtain information on its use and safety. Research studies done on humans, concluding that ultrasound is "safe," have been flawed, according to epidemiologists who specialize in study design. Since the current ultrasound equipment does not measure the intensity of ultrasound or the exposure time during an examination, it is difficult to compare and contrast results. Private practitioners and medical groups do not have to report the number and timing of prenatal ultrasound examinations, nor do they have to monitor women and their children to assess the long-term effects.

Nevertheless, the medical literature is beginning to show concern about the possibility of delayed or subtle manifestations of ultrasound exposure. Various associations have been made between fetal exposure to ultrasound and low birth weight. Some physicians believe that children exposed to ultrasound should be studied for nerve reflex changes, shortened attention spans, and behavioral or intelligence deficiencies. Given the remaining questions on its safety during pregnancy, the panel stated, "Diagnostic ultrasound is considered to be a low-risk procedure. However, routine use of ultrasound in pregnancy should be discouraged."

Long-Term Effects

Some doctors view ultrasound as overcoming the barrier between the fetus and the outside world (the barrier is the pregnant woman). They are enthusiastic about its use although long-term risks are not yet known. But if your health care provider performs ultrasound as a ritual of pregnancy, ask if s/he is aware of any side effects. If the provider insists there are no dangers or tries to reassure you that it will not harm you or your offspring, s/he may be unfamiliar with the medical literature or s/he may have decided that the benefits outweigh the risks. It is really too early to be sure. Remember that diethylstilbestrol (DES), an anti-miscarriage drug given to women decades ago, was originally considered safe. Twenty years later it was found to cause cancer and reproductive problems in children who were exposed to it prenatally. If you are concerned that your provider is not informed about the potential dangers of ultrasound, find a more knowledgeable practitioner or seek a second opinion about its need in your pregnancy.

As we have seen, ultrasound is useful in certain specific situations. Most health care providers focus on the positive aspects of the ultrasound examination. Some providers say it will help you bond to the fetus and perceive your pregnancy as real. But ultrasound technology can also have some unexpected psychological effects. Some women do get an enormous thrill from seeing the fetus. Others become very anxious about the pregnancy. For some women who later have the disabled fetus aborted, having "seen" it on ultrasound can be very upsetting.

You now know what the ultrasound process is. Before you choose to have or decline this procedure, read Book Three (p. 149), "To Test or Not to Test."

The following self-awareness exercise is meant only to help you clarify for yourself why you are considering the test.

The Choice for Ultrasound

A. Check your reasons for considering ultrasound.

☐ It will be thrilling to see the child and have its photograph.

☐ My doctor wants me to have it.

☐ I will learn my baby's sex.

☐ I will learn if I am having twins.

☐ My partner will see the fetus.

☐ I will know whether or not my due date is correct.

☐ My doctor can verify the position of my placenta.

☐ My doctor can check for certain unsuspected birth defects.

☐ I have decided to have amniocentesis and therefore ultrasound is necessary.

☐ I don't want to feel guilty that I did not take advantage of the technology.

B. Write down any other reasons.

_____

_____

_____

The Choice Against Ultrasound

A. Check your reasons for NOT wanting to have an ultrasound.

☐ I don't want unnecessary testing.

☐ I don't want to deal with the anxiety involved.

☐ I know approximately when my baby is due.

☐ I have no reason to believe that my baby is not developing normally.

☐ There is nothing I will do differently if I learn that I am having twins or that my baby has a disability.

☐ I don't want to see the baby and then be faced with the decision of having an abortion if an abnormality is found.

☐ My repeat MSAFP level was within the normal range.

B. Write down any other reasons.

_____

_____

_____

Now that you have clarified your own thinking about ultrasound, discuss it with your partner and your health care provider. Then consult the last section of this book (p. 149) for help in choosing or refusing this test.

6 | Amniocentesis

Amniocentesis (am′-nee-oh-sen-tee′-sis), sometimes referred to as an "amnio" or a "tap," has become a common procedure performed during pregnancy. In fact, amniocentesis has become so popular that many women feel it is as safe and easy as having a sample of blood drawn from the arm. Many women also think that amniocentesis will confirm that everything is fine in their pregnancy. Yet amniocentesis is much more complex than most people realize. A "normal" amniocentesis does not guarantee a "normal" baby at birth. It can only indicate whether the baby has the condition for which it is being tested.

WHAT IS AMNIOCENTESIS?

Amniocentesis is a surgical test in which a needle is inserted through the woman's abdomen into the womb to remove a sample of the amniotic fluid. The amniotic fluid contains cells and chemicals that are shed by the fetal skin and urinary tract. These substances can be analyzed to determine the genetic makeup of your baby. When amniocentesis is performed in the second trimester, it is often referred to as "prenatal genetic diagnosis."

USES OF AMNIOCENTESIS

Once your amniotic fluid is collected it is sent to a cytogenetics laboratory. There, it is fed with nutrients in order to enhance the growth of fetal cells. Growing a large number of cells is necessary to provide sufficient numbers to complete the tests. Once the cells have multiplied, they are removed from the fluid and the chromosomes within the cells (which contain the genetic information) are studied. This is known as a chromosome analysis. The fluid portion can be used for metabolic or biochemical tests.

Chromosome Analysis

Chromosome analysis looks at and identifies variations in the structure or number of chromosomes. The most common chromosome variation detected this way is trisomy 21, or Down syndrome. (See p. 211.)

A chromosome analysis will also reveal the sex of your baby. If you have an amnio, tell your health care provider whether or not you want to know if you are carrying a girl or a boy. Page 92 contains an exercise to help you decide what your reasons might be for having this information prenatally. Performing an amniocentesis solely for sex determination is not routinely done, unless you carry a gene for a particular disorder that will only affect one sex—for example, a gene for hemophilia which occurs mostly in males.

Amniotic Fluid Tests

A substance in the amniotic fluid called amniotic fluid alpha-fetoprotein (AFAFP) can be used to determine your baby's health. It passes from the baby's blood into your amniotic fluid where it can be measured. High levels of AFAFP may indicate the presence of open neural tube disorders such as spina bifida and anencephaly, or openings in the fetal stomach or intestines. If the AFAFP level is high, two other biochemicals, acetylcholinesterase (AChe) and hemoglobin F (HbF), are usually analyzed. If they also are high, there is almost certainly a variation in the fetus.

You need to remember, though, that elevated levels of AFAFP have been known to occur in other circumstances, when, for example, the amniotic needle inadvertently pokes the placenta or baby during the tap and the specimen is contaminated by fetal blood.

Metabolic and Biochemical Tests

Abnormalities in protein or chemical metabolism can sometimes be diagnosed by looking at the chemical makeup of the amniotic fluid or cells. Approximately seventy different metabolic disorders can be identified prenatally by metabolic tests, but because of expense and technical complications, these tests are usually only done on the amniotic fluid in instances where there is a family history of a metabolic disorder such as Tay-Sachs disease (see p. 217 in the appendix). If you are considering amniocentesis, ask your doctor what tests s/he has routinely performed on the fluid specimen and which tests would be done specifically for you.

DNA Studies

There are a number of experimental laboratory techniques to analyze DNA, the actual gene material within fetal cells. Laboratory tests are being developed to study genetic markers, substances that may indicate a variation in certain gene products. Testing for cystic fibrosis, sickle-cell anemia, thalassemia, and other blood disorders can be done with varying accuracy by specialized laboratories when these conditions are suspected.

AMNIO FOR WHOM?

Medical professionals generally recommend that amniocentesis be considered if the chance of having a child with a disability exceeds the risk of the amniocentesis procedure itself. (See p. 88 for a discussion of risk.) Some providers offer amnio to all of their clients; others do not. The practice of your provider will probably be influenced by her/his own personal, religious, and ethical beliefs and her/his concerns about liability. Meanwhile, the recommendations as to who should be offered amniocentesis are constantly expanding.

According to professional organizations, such as the American College of Obstetricians and Gynecologists and the National Society of Human Genetics, an amnio is recommended if one of the following conditions exist:

1. You have had an abnormal MSAFP level that is unexplained by ultrasound.

2. You have previously had a child with a disability that can be identified by this test.

3. You have had three or more miscarriages, or if your partner had a wife previously who had three or more miscarriages. (Some research suggests that half of all spontaneously aborted fetuses have a chromosomal variation and that this may be due to an inherited alteration in either the maternal or paternal genetic material.)

4. You and/or your partner are carriers for an inherited condition that can be detected in the fetus, for example, Tay-Sachs or sickle cell disease.

5. You are a carrier for a sex-linked (X-linked) disorder such as hemophilia or Duchenne muscular dystrophy. The gene for these disorders is carried by females and is usually expressed in males. Amniocentesis can also be used to identify the sex of your baby or to see if your fetus has this condition. This information may be useful to parents who are known carriers and would terminate the pregnancy of a male baby with a sex-linked disorder.

6. You or your partner have a known rearrangement (balanced translocation) of your chromosomes. People with a balanced translocation have a rearrangement of their chromosomes involving the attachment (or translocation) of all or part of one chromosome to another. The health of persons who are translocation carriers is not affected because their genetic material is rearranged evenly. However, people with translocation are thought to have an increased chance of passing on too much or too little chromosomal material to their children, though the effects can't always be predicted. The presence of a chromosome variation due to a balanced or unbalanced state in the fetus can almost always be detected via amniocentesis.

7. If you have been exposed to toxic environmental substances that are known to cause problems in unborn babies. It should be noted, though, that the information provided from amniocentesis may be very limited in this situation.

8. You are over the age of thirty-five. (See chapter 11: "Assessing Your Pregnancy 'Risk,' " for details on maternal age and chromosome variations.)

9. You have "excessive anxiety" about the health of your developing baby.

In addition to these criteria, however, in actual practice, many doctors see the main use of amniocentesis in early pregnancy as "confirming a normal pregnancy" or providing reassurance.

TIMING THE AMNIO

Amniocentesis for prenatal diagnosis is commonly performed between the sixteenth and eighteenth week of pregnancy. By sixteen weeks there is usually enough amniotic fluid, intrauterine space, and fetal cells to allow insertion of the amnio needle and withdrawal of the fluid.

Technically it may be possible to perform amniocentesis in the first trimester (between eleven and fourteen weeks), and a few researchers are experimenting with it at this stage. The basis for performing an "early amnio" is that the fluid volume has stabilized and the proportion of baby and placenta to the fluid allows enough room to insert the needle. New laboratory techniques are being developed which require only about one teaspoon of fluid to be drawn and which produce results within a week to ten days.

Since it can take up to three to five weeks to complete the cell studies, you may be between nineteen and twenty-one weeks at the time of the amnio results. If you plan to have an abortion—in the rare instance that a disorder is found—you will need remaining time to plan for it. To be safe, find out what the time limit is on performing a second-trimester abortion in your state.

Amniocentesis can also be done in the third trimester or at other times in your pregnancy when you want to know about your baby's health. If any problems are suspected late in your pregnancy, amniocentesis can be done to determine the presence of certain substances that will indicate maturity of the baby's lungs and its ability to breathe once it is born. If you have an amnio for this purpose, and did not have it earlier, the fetal cells and chromosomes can also be studied at this point.

COSTS OF AMNIO

The cost for an amniocentesis varies between $350 and $700. Some doctors charge for the entire prenatal genetic package, which might include genetic counseling, MSAFP screening, ultrasound, amniocentesis, and all laboratory tests. This can bring the total cost to between $800 and $1500.

Not all insurance companies will cover the cost of amniocentesis, but you should not be denied an amniocentesis because you can't afford it. In some states Medicaid covers the cost of amniocentesis. Get in touch with your state genetic service program (see appendix, pp. 246–251) for information about financial assistance for amniocentesis.

WHERE TO GO FOR AMNIOCENTESIS

If you elect to have amniocentesis, find an experienced doctor to do the test. Ask your doctor how many amnios s/he does—although the number alone is not the only indication of the physician's skill. Some doctors refer pregnant women to a genetics center where a geneticist or obstetrician who specializes in amniocentesis will perform the test. Before you make your decision, ask your doctor how many amnios s/he performs per week, per month, or per year. Perhaps you could talk with other women who have had this doctor do their "tap."

Special problems sometimes occur when the amnio is done in the doctor's office and the fluid is sent to an outside laboratory.

Better results are often obtained when samples are hand-carried to the lab than when they are mailed from the doctor's office. If the first analysis is not successful (for example, the cells do not grow in the laboratory), the amniocentesis may have to be repeated. If you are considering amniocentesis, ask your doctor how and where the amniotic fluid specimen is sent. By mail? By courier? You may want to transport it to the laboratory yourself if it is done in your doctor's office and then sent to an outside laboratory. Many genetic centers have laboratories on the premises. The closer you are to the laboratory, the greater your chances of having a successful cell culture on the first attempt.

To have an experienced laboratory is almost as important as to have an experienced doctor. In such a lab there is less chance of contaminating a culture or making a mistake. You may want to ask your provider about the lab's success rate for cell cultures from the first amniotic fluid. Some labs report as high as a 99 percent success rate. Also ask your doctor how long it will take to receive your amnio results. If it takes longer than four weeks, the lab being used is probably overextended. You might then want to consider having your sample sent elsewhere.

INFORMED CONSENT

If you decide to have this test, you will probably be asked to sign a form stating that you understand the risks and benefits and you agree to the amnio procedure.

PREPARATION FOR AMNIO

For many women the thought of a long needle entering their womb causes great concern and anxiety. A normal response to this type of stress is to tighten or contract the abdominal muscles during the procedure. This reflex can cause further physical and emotional tension and possibly make the uterine muscles so tense that you may have to reschedule the amnio.

If you do choose to have an amniocentesis, prepare yourself by practicing various relaxation techniques. Prior to your amnio, try to practice breathing and relaxation exercises to do during your prenatal tests.

Besides practicing relaxation techniques, ask your partner to be with you during the actual amnio procedure. Your partner may be able to provide moral support and physical comfort for you. This type of involvement and presence will help you feel that your pregnancy is a shared experience. Obviously, invite your partner to be with you only if that will make you feel more calm.

PRE-AMNIO ULTRASOUND

A diagnostic ultrasound should always be done just before you have amniocentesis. The pre-amnio ultrasound will (1) accurately assess the age of your baby; (2) establish if you are carrying more than one baby; (3) assess the shape and position of your uterus; (4) rule out any abnormality that could cause a complication during the amnio procedure; and (5) determine a spot on your abdomen for placement of the amnio needle.

The ultrasound is usually kept on during the entire amniocentesis procedure so that the position of your placenta and the baby are visible during the insertion of the needle and the withdrawal of fluid. Some doctors will do an ultrasound before the amniocentesis, but then turn off the ultrasound machine while the "tap" is actually being done, and turn it back on afterwards. Doctors have even been known to have women walk from the room where the ultrasound was done to the "amnio room." This can be extremely dangerous because the fetus can move around and change positions quickly. Ask the doctor performing the amniocentesis if s/he uses continuous ultrasound.

TWINS AND AMNIO

If you are carrying twins and you are considering amniocentesis, be sure to use an experienced doctor who has performed many amnios on women with a twin pregnancy. An amniocentesis in the presence of twins is a difficult procedure.

If the twins are fraternal, there will be two separate amniotic sacs. The obstetrician will have to inject a dye into one sac so s/he will know if the same sac has been inadvertently tapped twice. If you are carrying identical twins there will only be a single sac. Since identical twins almost always share the same genetic information, a single puncture is most often adequate.

Many women who have twins express apprehension at the thought of amniocentesis. They are concerned not only with the risks of the procedure, but also with the question of what they will do if the amnio reveals an abnormality in one twin only. Some women with one healthy and one abnormal twin have opted to terminate their pregnancy. Others have opted to carry both twins to term and to raise one or both. Other women attempt to terminate the abnormal fetus while allowing the normal fetus to carry to term. The latter procedure, known as selective abortion or termination of twins, is still experimental.

PRE-AMNIO MSAFP SCREENING TEST

If you choose to have amniocentesis, you may also have a pre-amnio maternal serum alpha-fetoprotein (MSAFP) blood sample drawn immediately prior to the amnio procedure. This is done to correlate the blood and amniotic fluid alpha-fetoprotein (AFAFP). Sometimes the pre-amnio MSAFP level is elevated but the AFAFP level is normal. Although the relationship between these two remains speculative, some researchers suggest that an elevated pre-amnio MSAFP level in the presence of a normal AFAFP level may be a sign that a baby will be born prematurely. (See chapter 4 on the MSAFP screening test for more information.)

KNOWING YOUR BLOOD TYPE

Before you have an amnio, know your blood type. If you are Rh-negative and the father is Rh-positive, you may want to receive an injection of Rh-immune globulin. Otherwise, if some of the fetal blood enters your circulation, an incompatibility could result that could harm your baby.

THE AMNIO PROCEDURE

If you choose to have amniocentesis, you will be asked to lie flat on your back on a narrow table. You will have to expose your abdomen, so it is best to wear a shirt and slacks rather than a dress. Your doctor, wearing sterile gloves, will put a sterile sheet above and below your abdomen. S/he will then clean your abdominal area with a cold, wet antiseptic solution. Sometimes a local anesthetic, such as xylocaine, will be injected near the place of the needle insertion. Many doctors do not use an anesthetic because they claim the procedure is "not very painful." Depending on the doctor, this is another one of your choices: if you would prefer an anesthetic, let your provider know.

Once your abdomen is "prepped," the doctor will pass an amnio needle approximately three and a half inches long through your abdomen, through your uterine muscle, through the amniotic sac, to the amniotic fluid, or the bag of water. A syringe is then attached to the needle, and one or two teaspoonfuls of fluid are withdrawn. The amniotic fluid should be colorless and odorless. If a greenish fluid is aspirated it could mean that the fetus, understandably under stress, had a bowel movement, or, less commonly, the needle punctured the baby's small bowel. If blood is aspirated it may mean that a maternal blood vessel was punctured, or, less commonly, the needle punctured a fetal blood vessel.

Sometimes several needle insertions will be necessary to obtain a sufficient amount of amniotic fluid. If this occurs, a new needle should be used each time, but it is generally believed that there should not be more than two needle insertions during an amniocentesis.

Once enough amniotic fluid is drawn, the needle is removed, the amniotic fluid is put in a test tube, and the amniocentesis is over. Some doctors will put a bandage on your abdomen to cover the procedure site. The amniotic fluid, which is made by the baby's urine, is usually replaced within a few hours.

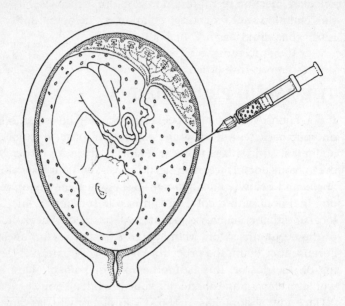

With the high volume of amniocenteses now being done, samples can be mixed up or mislabeled. Watch to see that your name is written on your tube of amniotic fluid. If the amnio is being done in your doctor's office, you may want to suggest that you can hand-deliver it to the laboratory to avoid any problems in transport.

In some instances your doctor may be unable to obtain any amniotic fluid. This can occur if your uterine muscle contracts as the needle is being inserted (a normal reaction to a foreign object) or if there is not enough amniotic fluid at the time of testing. If an amniocentesis is unsuccessful after two attempts, you will want to decide whether to repeat the test. If so, you will probably have to reschedule the test a few days to one week later.

AFTER THE AMNIO

After amniocentesis your baby's heart movements should be carefully observed on the ultrasound machine. Your doctor will probably give you specific instructions on such matters as activity, exercise, and lovemaking. If s/he does not, ask what precautions are appropriate.

After the procedure you should be on the lookout for any rise in your temperature or leakage of amniotic fluid or blood, either abdominally where the needle was inserted or vaginally.

Although many physicians do not think that any change in schedule is necessary after the amnio procedure, many women naturally want to rest after the procedure. This can contribute to your general physical and emotional well-being. If you have been under stress about the test (which many women are, whether or not they are consciously aware of it), your body will appreciate having time to rest.

RECEIVING AMNIO RESULTS

Ask your health care provider how you will be notified about your amnio results. If your provider sends your amniotic fluid sample to an outside laboratory, the laboratory should notify your provider immediately of all abnormal test results. If you feel anxious or in suspended animation during the waiting period, request that you be informed immediately by phone of the test results, whether normal or abnormal.

NORMAL RESULTS

Most women who have amniocentesis receive normal results. In order to interpret that, you should know what conditions were being tested for. Usually a normal result means that your baby has the normal size, shape, and number of chromosomes (twenty-two pairs or forty-four autosomes), and two gender-related chromosomes—either XX for female or XY for male. This means that the baby probably does not have a chromosome variation. If the amniotic fluid, AFP, is normal, it means the baby probably does not have an open neural tube disorder.

NORMAL VARIATIONS

A number of fetal chromosomal variations have not been associated with any clinical effects in the fetus. For example, certain inversions on a chromosome (INV9), dark stains in certain places on one chromosome (QHPLUS), or extra material on a Y chromosome (XYQPLUS) may be normal variants and not significant. This is another anxiety-provoking situation that you may want to be prepared for if you have an amnio.

ABNORMAL RESULTS

In the rare circumstance that an abnormal finding is identified, different cells from different Petri dishes will be examined to confirm the result. If the variation appears consistently, you will be told that your fetus has whatever condition is indicated.

Amniocentesis is testing for variations in chromosomes, biochemical or metabolic variations, and changes in DNA. You could be told that the test reveals a chromosome condition such as Down syndrome, a biochemical variation such as spina bifida, a metabolic deficiency such as Tay-Sachs, or a blood disorder. (See appendix, p. 211, for a description of disabilities.) Bear in mind that the fluid may not have been analyzed for all these potential conditions. Your results will be only as complete as the tests.

Because amniocentesis is not always perfect, you need to understand that a baby can be born with a disability after a "normal amniocentesis." There is also the chance that a healthy baby may be incorrectly identified as having a disability.

Whatever the "abnormal" results, you should not be pushed into an immediate decision. Think carefully about the implications of the results. There may be other confirmatory procedures such as the PUBS test (see chapter 8), involving direct acquisition of fetal blood versus the fetal cells that have been shed into the amniotic fluid. (See chapter 10 if you receive abnormal results.)

ACCURACY OF AMNIOCENTESIS

Amniocentesis is considered highly accurate. However, numerous problems can occur in the laboratory that might affect your test results. These include the following:

Maternal Cell Contamination

Sometimes cells from the pregnant woman are unintentionally picked up in the syringe during amniocentesis. This contamination can make the interpretation of the fetus's chromosomes inaccurate. Sometimes only the mother's cells are cultured. It can be especially difficult to know whose cells are being analyzed if your fetus is female. Under these circumstances, if there is a variation in a cell line, you don't know if it reflects the genetic makeup of the fetus or the mother. If your results show such a variation, you can do one of three things: nothing, repeat the amnio, or consider having the PUBS test described in chapter 8 to confirm or dismiss this finding. Maternal cell contamination is also known as "maternal cell admixture."

Cell Culture Failure

Sometimes the cells fail to multiply in the laboratory. This does not mean your baby has an increased chance of having a disability, but rather that the sample size was insufficient or something went wrong in the laboratory processing procedure. Your doctor may or may not be up front about this, but if the cells don't "grow," you may choose to repeat the amniocentesis or have the PUBS test so that you will have your results before whatever the legal date is in your state for terminating a pregnancy, if that would be your choice. If this type of laboratory error occurs, you can also refuse to repeat the test.

Artifact

Growing fetal cells in a Petri dish in the laboratory sometimes gives results that do not represent the true genetic makeup of the fetus. These results, called artifacts, appear in the lab but do not exist in your baby. An example of this is something called pseudomosaicism. In this case, all the cells in the culture do not reproduce themselves exactly. The laboratory analysis will show some cells with one type of chromosome constituency, other cells with another.

True mosaicism, where more than one cell line is present, sometimes really does occur in the population, but it is extremely rare. Most so-called mosaicisms in an amniotic fluid culture are "pseudo," or false. If your doctor reports this finding you will have a difficult choice to make. You can either choose or refuse to repeat the amnio, or have the PUBS test (see chapter 8) to confirm or dismiss this type of finding.

RISKS

Most health professionals and consumer literature maintain that amniocentesis in early pregnancy is a safe procedure. The assertion of safety is largely based on a nationwide study sponsored by the National Institute of Child Health and Human Development (NICHD) done in 1976. The commonly cited statistic is that fetal loss is 0.5 percent. However, others cite a fetal loss of 1 percent to 1.5 percent from amniocentesis. A recent journal article from Denmark, describing a study that followed the pregnancy of women twenty-five to thirty-four, found that those who had amniocentesis were 2.3 times as likely to have a spontaneous abortion as those who did not. In addition, respiratory distress syndrome and pneumonia occurred more frequently when the mother had amniocentesis.

The long-term effects of amniocentesis are not fully understood. The safety of amniocentesis is influenced by the skill of the doctor performing the test and your individual circumstances.

Infection

You can develop an infection of your amniotic sac if any of the equipment becomes contaminated before or during the procedure. Infections may also occur for other unknown reasons. As I mentioned earlier, after each amnio attempt the needle should be discarded and a new sterile one should be attached to the syringe. An infection to the amniotic sac can be a potentially devastating complication. After your amnio you may want to take your temperature every four to six hours for approximately twenty-four hours, so that if a fever does occur you can treat it immediately. If you develop any signs of fever, such as warmth or shaking chills, inform your health care provider right away.

Abdominal Leaks
A little bleeding may occur at the puncture site following the amnio. Usually a bandage will stop it. Sometimes amniotic fluid will seep out of the puncture site on the abdomen. Amniotic fluid is clear and odorless. If there is leakage it indicates that the amniotic membrane has not been sealed. Amniotic fluid leakage or any bleeding should be reported immediately to your health care provider. Although the opening generally will seal itself within a few hours, an opening even the size of a pinpoint can be a source of infection.

Bleeding
Vaginal bleeding or spotting are abnormal and should be reported immediately to your health care provider. Bleeding does not necessarily mean that you will miscarry. It may indicate that a blood vessel in the uterus was nicked by the needle during the procedure. Occasionally the uterine muscle contracts so forcefully after the amnio needle is inserted that the placenta begins to separate (also known as *abruptio placentae*), and bleeding and, potentially, a miscarriage can occur.

Isoimmunization
If there is a blood incompatibility between you and your baby, a reaction can occur as a result of the amniocentesis. Therefore, your blood type and that of the baby's father should be determined before the procedure. If there is a blood incompatibility, a medication called Rhogam will be given to you by injection after the amnio procedure. (See appendix, p. 211, for information on Rh disease.)

Harm to the Baby
Many women are concerned about the chance of the needle injuring their baby during amniocentesis. Fortunately, most unborn babies have a natural instinct to pull away from foreign objects like an amnio needle when it enters their protected environment.

Furthermore, with the use of sophisticated ultrasound machinery, during the amniocentesis a skilled clinician can usually determine the appropriate place to insert the needle to avoid touching the fetus.

If the needle does touch the baby, there may be no harm done. One doctor recently told me about a fetus that was stretching as the amniocentesis was performed. The baby's heel pressed against the needle. When she examined the baby at birth, she found "not a mark." Others have noted "dimples" in areas thought to have come in contact with the amnio needle, but there was nothing conclusive. Obviously, any degree of disability would depend on what the needle inadvertently touches. There has been speculation that certain disabilities, such as limb deficiencies, can result from this test. Amniotic bands, lines of scar tissue, have been noted on placentas of some women who have had this test. If this scar tissue forms, it can restrict the space within the uterus and might affect fetal growth.

Miscarriage

Losing a baby as a result of an elective procedure during pregnancy is a devastating experience. Although extremely rare, miscarriage is a complication that can and does occur, when, for example, there is a rupture of the amniotic sac or irritation to the muscle of the uterus.

The chance of miscarriage is said to be "not statistically significant." Despite population-based calculations you may still want to make an independent decision. It could help to know your own health care provider's "miscarriage rate" as a result of amniocentesis. Ask yourself the following questions: What risks can I accept? What would be more difficult to deal with, a naturally occurring miscarriage or a miscarriage after amniocentesis? Talk with your partner, your provider, and other women about how they made their decisions to amnio or not to amnio.

You now know what the amniocentesis process is. Before you choose to have or decline this procedure, read Book Three, "To Test or Not to Test."

The following self-awareness exercise is meant only to help you clarify for yourself why you are considering the test.

The Choice for Amniocentesis

A. Check your reasons for considering amniocentesis.

☐ I am concerned about the health of my baby.

☐ I or the baby's father has a medical condition or a family history of a disability, such as a birth defect, inherited disorder, chromosome abnormality, sex-linked disease, or mental retardation.

☐ I have a disability myself that puts me at high risk.

☐ I previously have had a baby with a disability.

☐ The results will help me plan for the care of my baby after it is born.

☐ The results will help me decide for or against abortion if the fetus has a disability.

☐ I was thirty-five years of age or older when I conceived.

☐ My doctor wants me to have it.

☐ My partner wants me to have it.

☐ I don't want to feel guilty that I didn't take advantage of the available technology.

☐ I work with substances that may affect the health of my unborn baby.

B. Write down any other reasons.

_____

_____

_____

The Choice Against Amniocentesis

A. Check your reasons for NOT wanting amnio.

☐ The risk of the procedure is higher than the chance that my baby has a disability.

☐ I have no reason to believe that my baby is not developing normally.

☐ I don't want unnecessary testing.

☐ There is nothing I would do differently if I learned that my baby has a disability.

B. Write down any other reasons.

_____

_____

_____

IS IT A GIRL OR A BOY?

Think about whether you are considering amniocentesis in order to determine the sex of your unborn baby. What are your own expectations for your baby? Try to describe your dream child: Is it a boy or a girl?

What Color Hair? What Color Eyes?

How do you think you might feel if you learn your dream child differs from the baby that's growing inside you? Will you be able to accept the child on its own terms? If you or your partner desires a child of a certain gender, what would you do if your child refuses to cooperate?

Some few women have had an abortion because their baby was not the desired sex. How do you feel about using modern technology for this purpose?

The Choice for Amnio to Determine the Sex of the Fetus

A. Check your reasons for testing for gender.

☐ The technology is available, and it would be fun to know.

☐ I will be able to name my baby *in utero.*

☐ I can terminate my pregnancy if the baby is not the sex I want.

☐ I am the carrier of a sex-linked disease that affects males.

B. Write down any other reasons.

_____

_____

_____

Now that you have clarified your own thinking about amnio, discuss it with your partner and your health care provider. Then consult Book Three (p. 149) for help in choosing or refusing this test.

7 | Chorionic Villus Sampling (CVS)

A new and still experimental prenatal test is receiving attention as an alternative to amniocentesis. The name of the test is chorionic villus sampling (CVS), once referred to as chorionic villus biopsy (CVB). CVS is sometimes referred to by the medical profession as "the career woman's prenatal diagnosis" because it provides an earlier result for a pregnant woman than amniocentesis.

Chorionic villus sampling originated in China for the purpose of identifying fetal sex. Abortion of female fetuses was most often the result of this method of population control. Within the past decade, however, CVS has been promoted and used as a means of identifying fetal disabilities in the United States and Europe.

WHAT IS CVS?

CVS is an early surgical test that removes from the uterus a piece of chorion, the outer tissue of the sac surrounding the embryo. The chorion is then analyzed to determine the genetic makeup of the fetus.

Chorionic villus sampling can diagnose certain genetic disorders in the fetus at nine to twelve weeks during the first trimester.

Although CVS is still experimental, some researchers predict that it will soon replace second-trimester amniocentesis.

Many women feel that getting information early in the pregnancy about a disability in the fetus means that they can make decisions before other people even know they are pregnant. Also, because the test is performed early enough so that they haven't already felt the baby move, they may not have developed the closeness that may come by the second trimester. Each woman must weigh these advantages of early prenatal diagnosis against the risks that accompany the test.

If you are considering CVS during your pregnancy, it is important to know that the safety, accuracy, and long-term effects of this procedure are still being evaluated. There is even some question about the extent to which the tissue that is sampled accurately reflects the genetic makeup of the fetus.

A normal CVS in the first trimester doesn't mean you can relax for the rest of your pregnancy. The truth is that you still will have to decide about other prenatal testing in later pregnancy for conditions CVS does not address.

USES OF CVS

Chorionic villus sampling tests for many of the same disabilities as amniocentesis, but not all of them. It is used for (1) chromosomal studies to identify chromosome conditions, such as Down syndrome; (2) biochemical studies to look for conditions that affect metabolism, such as Tay-Sachs disease; (3) DNA studies to look for conditions that have a specific pattern of inheritance, such as cystic fibrosis, Duchenne muscular dystrophy, thalassemia, or sickle-cell anemia; and (4) determining whether the fetus is male or female (see p. 92). It cannot identify the presence of neural tube conditions, such as spina bifida.

CVS FOR WHOM?

Since chorionic villus sampling is thought to provide information similar to that provided by amniocentesis, doctors suggest that women who might choose amniocentesis fall into the same category as those who might choose CVS. This means that CVS could be an option for you if one of the following conditions exist:

1) You have had a previous child with a disability that can be diagnosed by CVS.

2) You and/or your partner are carriers for an inherited condition that can be detected in the fetus, such as Tay-Sachs or sickle-cell disease.

3) You are a carrier for a sex-linked (X-linked) disorder, such as hemophilia or Duchenne muscular dystrophy. (The genes for these conditions are carried by females and are usually expressed in males. CVS is used to identify the sex of the baby when a female may be a carrier.)

4) You or your partner has a known balanced translocation of your chromosomes. People with a balanced translocation have a rearrangement of their chromosomes, involving the attachment (or translocation) of all or part of one chromosome to another. Because their genetic material is rearranged evenly, the health of persons who are translocation carriers is not affected. However, people with translocation are thought to have an increased chance of passing on too much or too little chromosomal material to their children, though the effects can't always be predicted. The presence of a chromosome variation due to a balanced or unbalanced state in the fetus can almost always be detected via CVS.

5) You are over the age of thirty-five. (Some doctors will not perform CVS for this reason. They feel the risk of miscarriage from the test may be greater than the chance of having an infant with a chromosome problem. Other doctors offer CVS to women of all ages.)

WHEN NOT TO DO CVS

It's probably safest not to have chorionic villus sampling if (1) you are carrying more than one fetus; (2) you have had bleeding from your uterus during pregnancy; (3) you have an active genital herpes infection; (4) you have uterine fibroids which could make access to the chorion difficult; and (5) your cervical canal is angled in such a way that it would not allow safe passage of the catheter. (In this situation the transabdominal approach would also be better.)

TIMING THE TEST

Although experience with chorionic villus sampling is limited, the best time seems to be from nine to twelve weeks (first trimester) instead of sixteen to twenty weeks (second trimester), when amniocentesis is performed. Earlier than nine weeks there may be a problem obtaining an adequate amount of tissue, and risks of the procedure increase. Furthermore, most spontaneous abortions occur during the first trimester, and there is fear that CVS might be associated with these abortions.

If you are traveling some distance to have CVS, try to calculate the age of your pregnancy as carefully as possible, using the date of your last menstrual period (see p. 33). Otherwise you may be asked to return at a later date.

COSTS OF CVS

The cost of CVS ranges between $800 and $1500, including genetic counseling, ultrasound, and laboratory tests. Because CVS is still experimental, some insurance companies will not cover the costs of this test.

CVS VERSUS AMNIO

In some centers performing CVS, you must commit to having an abortion if the test result is abnormal. If you plan to keep the baby despite test results, you may not be a candidate for CVS. (Of course, you are entitled to change your mind at any time.) When you choose amniocentesis to obtain information about fetal health, you can choose abortion or plan for specialized care of a disabled baby during and after birth.

If, however, a disability is diagnosed by CVS, women can have a first-trimester abortion which they cannot do with amnio, which is performed later in the pregnancy. In general, procedures for first-trimester abortions are thought to carry fewer physical risks and cause less psychological trauma than those done in the second trimester. (See chapter 10 for details on abortion.)

WHERE TO GO FOR CVS

Chorionic villus sampling can be performed in a outpatient clinic or in a doctor's office. The procedure requires an experienced obstetrician who has had extensive training in CVS. An experienced ultrasonographer should also be part of the team. Because the maternal cells need to be separated from the fetal cells after the procedure, some obstetricians have a skilled laboratory technician present to do this.

Just because your obstetrician says "I've done many amnios," or "I've aspirated many ovarian follicles, therefore I know the anatomy," doesn't necessarily mean that s/he is skilled in CVS. If you are considering having CVS, it's reasonable to ask your doctor how many procedures s/he has performed and in what settings. Be certain to ask about the complication rates and the outcomes of the various pregnancies. You may also want to speak to another woman who chose to have this procedure performed by the practitioner you are considering using.

Some states prohibit the procedure because it violates regulations related to fetal experimentation. Because of this, women have flown across the country for CVS. Obviously, an experienced laboratory is almost as important as an experienced doctor.

INFORMED CONSENT

If you decide to have this test, you will be asked to sign a form stating that you agree to the CVS procedure. The test is still considered experimental and the catheter used for the test is still being evaluated by the Food and Drug Administration (FDA).

BEFORE CVS

If you choose to have the CVS procedure, you will be asked for the results of the routine vaginal tests done at your first prenatal visit to screen for infectious diseases like gonorrhea or chlamydia, and information on your blood type. If you are Rh-negative and the father is Rh-positive, an injection of Rhogam immune globulin will be recommended. Otherwise, if some fetal blood enters your circulation, an incompatibility may result that may harm your baby.

PREPARATION FOR CVS

For many women the thought of a suction catheter entering their womb causes great concern and anxiety. A normal response to this type of stress is to tighten or contract the perineal muscles during the procedure. This reflex can cause further physical and emotional tension and possibly make you so tense that you may have to reschedule the procedure.

If you do choose to have a CVS, prepare yourself by practicing various techniques to use during your prenatal tests to lessen tension, such as controlled breathing and muscle-relaxation exercises.

Besides practicing relaxation techniques, ask your partner to be with you during the actual CVS procedure. Your partner may be able to provide moral support and physical comfort as well as, by being present and involved, help you feel that your pregnancy is a shared experience. Obviously, invite your partner to be with you only if that will make you feel more calm.

PRE-CVS ULTRASOUND

A diagnostic ultrasound should always be done just before you have CVS. The pre-CVS ultrasound will (1) accurately assess the age of your baby; (2) establish if you are carrying more than one baby; (3) assess the shape and position of your uterus; (4) rule out any abnormality that could cause a complication during the procedure; and (5) determine where to guide the catheter.

The ultrasound will be kept on during the entire CVS procedure so that the position of your placenta and the baby are visible during the insertion of the catheter and the suctioning of tissue.

THE CVS PROCEDURE

Each of the several techniques used for CVS is based on obtaining a piece of chorion to study in the laboratory. Chorion is the outer tissue of the sac that surrounds the embryo inside the uterus during the first two months of pregnancy. The chorion is covered with fingerlike projections of tissue, called *villi,* which actually look like the surface of a shag rug or a well-kept lawn. These villi eventually form the placenta. During CVS, some of these villi are removed.

Although no one is certain what part of the chorionic villi is most suitable to remove for testing, many researchers feel that the "healthiest" villi are those in the center of the chorion where the placenta eventually forms. The villi in the periphery of the chorion disintegrate quickly and may not reflect the genetic makeup of the fetus. There have been situations described in the medical literature where a woman's fetus was diagnosed with a chromosome problem by one doctor and other doctors felt that it might just be an abnormality of the chorionic membrane, rather than the fetus. In some instances the woman carried the fetus to term, and indeed the fetus was healthy. Others have been told the fetus was healthy, when in fact a disability was present.

Vaginal CVS

CVS originally began as a "blind" technique. Without seeing where they were going, doctors would insert a long hollow tube called a *cannula,* or catheter, through the vagina and cervix. Then a piece of tissue, hopefully part of the chorionic villi, would be removed. Needless to say, this technique was extremely risky for a woman and her baby. Although it is no longer performed this way in the United States, women in the Third World are still being subjected to this dangerous practice.

"Direct vision" CVS enables the physician to see what s/he is doing. The doctor inserts an instrument (a hysteroscope) through an incision in the abdomen or through the cervix (using a fetoscope) and views the tissue. Following the insertion of the scope,

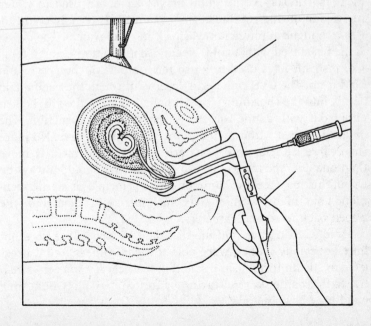

another tube is inserted through the abdomen or cervix, and the doctor biopsies, or cuts, a piece of the chorionic villus with very fine forceps. This method also requires that the doctor have very good vision, a steady hand, and superb skill. Even so, this method often yields an insufficient amount of tissue to study in the laboratory.

"Ultrasound-guided aspiration" has become the most common CVS technique in Europe and the United States. In this type of CVS procedure, you will be asked to lie on your back on a narrow table, and to place your hips at the end and your legs in stirrups (this is the lithotomy position used for routine pelvic exams). The doctor will then perform a bi-manual pelvic exam, inserting two fingers (covered with a glove and lubricating jelly) of one hand into the vaginal canal to hold the cervix. This will be done while the lights are out and the ultrasound machine is on so that the position of your uterus, fetus, and placenta can be seen on the screen.

After the pelvic exam a speculum will be lubricated with jelly and inserted into the vagina. A speculum is the metal instrument that looks like a double-hinged shoehorn used to widen the vagina during routine vaginal exams. It is usually cold (unless a thoughtful physician warms it in tepid water). The cervix is then cleansed with a cold, wet antiseptic solution, and a tong-like instrument is used to grasp the top part of the cervix and hold it up. The CVS catheter is inserted through the vagina and cervix into the chorionic villi. A small amount of the villi is then either cut with a fine forceps or aspirated using suction. The catheter is then withdrawn and the procedure is over. No more than three catheter insertions are usually performed. If more than one attempt is necessary, a new catheter should always be used. This may seem a common-sense principle of sterile technique, but many woman have had infections that could be traced back to reused catheters.

Some women have told me that the CVS procedure does not hurt, especially if they were able to relax. Others found it extremely uncomfortable and said that their cervix was very sensitive to the manipulation. Having a partner or friend to hold your hand may be calming.

Abdominal CVS

There is a new technique being used for CVS called "trans-abdominal CVS." The procedure is much like amniocentesis (p. 83) using ultrasound guidance. It involves inserting a needle through the abdomen directly into the center of the chorion to remove the villi. The position of the chorion/placenta is important when considering CVS. If the chorion is anterior (on the inside of the front of the uterus), sticking a needle through the abdomen may be easier than guiding a tube through the cervix and around to the abdominal area. However, if the chorion is posterior (on the inside of the back of the uterus), a trans-abdominal approach may be more difficult.

Though more information is necessary to compare the risks and benefits of each procedure, some doctors feel that the trans-abdominal approach to CVS is preferable to going through the cervix because it "bypasses the dirty vagina" (*dirty* meaning not sterile), thereby perhaps reducing the possibility of infection. It also requires less manipulation and poses less risk of injuring the fetus, chorion, and uterus, but the quality of the villi sample is still under question.

After CVS

After the CVS procedure your baby's heartbeat should be carefully observed on the ultrasound machine. Your doctor will give you specific instructions regarding such things as activity, exercise, and lovemaking. If s/he does not, ask what precautions are appropriate.

After the procedure you should be on the lookout for any rise in temperature or leakage of amniotic fluid (which is clear and odorless) or blood, because this could indicate possible complications of the test. Vaginal spotting or staining that is blood-tinged may occur after the procedure because of injury by the catheter to the sensitive walls of the vaginal canal. Avoid using tampons and try not to put anything into the vaginal area. To minimize danger of infection, women should probably avoid having internal vaginal exams unless necessary.

Although many physicians do not think that any change in schedule is necessary after the CVS procedure, many women naturally want to rest. This can contribute to your general physical and emotional well-being. If you have been under stress about the test—which many women are, whether or not they are aware of it—your body may appreciate having time to rest.

RECEIVING CVS RESULTS

A number of laboratory techniques are used to process chorionic villi depending on the diagnosis required. Chromosomes can be obtained from the cells while they are still dividing within the villi twenty-four to forty-eight hours after the sample is taken. Until recently, laboratories were able to complete a chromosome analysis from this "direct" method within a few days, but because of their concerns about accuracy, another technique is used to culture a greater number of cells in the laboratory. With this "indirect" approach a diagnosis can be made within a week or longer.

Some laboratories provide preliminary results from the direct analysis and confirm them later using the indirect method. This is probably the best approach since it is possible to miss certain abnormalities with the direct approach alone.

If biochemical studies are to be done, extracts of the chorionic villi may be prepared by the same methods used to prepare cultured amniotic fluid cells. DNA analysis performed on the chorionic villi can take a few weeks.

Ask your health care provider how you will be notified about your CVS results. If your provider sends your tissue to an outside laboratory, the laboratory should notify your provider immediately of all abnormal test results. If you feel anxious or in suspended animation during the waiting period, request that you be notified immediately by phone with the test results, whether they are normal or abnormal.

NORMAL CVS RESULTS

Most women who have CVS receive normal results. In order to interpret that, you should know what conditions were being tested for. Usually a normal result means that your baby has the proper size, shape, and number of chromosomes (twenty-two pairs or forty-four autosomes) and two gender-related chromosomes (either XX for female or XY for male). This means the baby probably does not have a chromosome variation. Because this test does not analyze amniotic fluid substances, it does not test for neural tube conditions.

VARIATIONS

A number of fetal chromosomal variations have not been associated with any clinical effects in the fetus. For example, certain inversions on a chromosome (INV9), dark stains in certain places of one chromosome (QHPLUS), or extra material on a Y chromosome (XYQHPLUS), may be normal variants and not significant. This is another anxiety-provoking situation that you may want to be prepared for if you have CVS.

ABNORMAL CVS RESULTS

In the rare circumstance that an abnormal finding is identified, you will probably be told that your fetus has whatever condition is indicated.

CVS is testing for variations in chromosomes or metabolic substances and in changes in DNA. You could be told that the test reveals a chromosome condition such as Down syndrome, a metabolic deficiency such as in PKU, or a blood disorder. Bear in mind that the tissue may not have been analyzed for all these potential conditions. Your results will be only as complete as the test.

Because CVS is not always perfect, you need to understand that a baby can be born with a disability after a "normal CVS." There is also the chance that a healthy baby may be incorrectly identified as having a disability.

Whatever the "abnormal" results, you should not be pushed into an immediate decision. Think carefully about the implications of the results. There may be other confirmatory procedures, such as an amniocentesis or the PUBS test (see chapter 8).

ACCURACY OF CVS

The accuracy of CVS is being currently debated. No one is sure that the chorionic tissue accurately reflects the genetic status of the fetus. Abnormal cell lines have been found in the chorionic tissue but not in fetal tissue. This means that there can be changes in the chorionic tissue that will not be present in your baby. These false abnormalities can also occur in cells collected from amniotic fluid, but they occur more frequently using CVS. As with all new laboratory tests, unforeseen, unexplained, and unrecognized errors occur. There are other factors that can occur in the laboratory and that might affect your results.

Also, after chorionic villi have been removed, the fetal tissue needs to be separated from maternal tissue to obtain an accurate diagnosis. Delays in the laboratory between the time you have the procedure and when the lab obtains the specimen are a common problem and may affect results, though the optimum time to obtain an accurate diagnosis is not known. Even when the separation or laboratory work is done correctly, the tissue sample may not be adequate or the preparation of the chromosomes in the laboratory may be of poor quality and unusable.

RISKS

CVS has been presented as a "painless procedure . . . done in a doctor's office . . . as early as the sixth week of pregnancy with risks probably the same as in midtrimester amniocentesis." This description minimizes the possible complications that can and do occur.

Infection

Infection is a frequent complication of CVS. A recently recognized flu-like syndrome—fever and muscle aches—following CVS can progress to a generalized infection (septicemia). If the infection is not managed appropriately with systemic antibiotics, it can be life-threatening. Some women have required hospitalization in an intensive-care unit because of the severity of the postprocedure infection. A high fever (our body's natural defense against infection) can lead to hypothermia, which may also be a cause of miscarriage. The therapeutic treatment of the complications themselves has been known to adversely affect the baby so that a woman may end up losing it or terminating an otherwise normal pregnancy.

Bleeding

Vaginal bleeding or spotting is abnormal and should be reported immediately to your health care provider. Bleeding does not necessarily mean that you will miscarry. It may indicate that a blood vessel was nicked during the procedure. Bleeding can occur if the placenta separates from the uterine wall or the uterus is perforated during the test. There has already been a situation in which a woman's uterus had to be removed because of complications in the CVS procedure.

Harm to Your Fetus

Although there is little definite information about fetal injury as a result of this test, CVS has been implicated in the cause of disabilities such as limb deficiencies. Upon examination of the placenta after birth, amniotic bands (fine bands of tissue that can restrict tissue growth) have been found. Researchers suggested that these amniotic bands may have been caused by the CVS procedure.

Cervical Lacerations

Once the cannula is guided through the cervix, there can be problems placing it in the right site. Sometimes, when manipulating the catheter through the cervix, cervical lacerations, or tears, result.

Miscarriage

Other complications of CVS include rupture of the amniotic sac, causing a spontaneous abortion, or miscarriage. Some studies suggest a fetal loss rate between 1 percent and 5 percent, compared with .2 percent fetal-loss rate with amniocentesis. Some researchers disagree with attributing such a high fetal-loss rate to the procedure itself. They justify the high fetal-loss rate by saying that the rate of miscarriage in early pregnancy is unknown and that many of the miscarriages that occur after the procedure would have happened anyhow.

Long-Term Effects
The long-term effects of CVS are still unknown. The number of women who have had this prenatal test and have actually delivered a baby at term is relatively low. Researchers assume that removing villi will have no effect on a baby's development, but there is a possibility that removing a piece of the tissue that would eventually have become the placenta, the baby's lifeline, might have effects we are not yet aware of. More information about CVS needs to be collected and correlated with such factors as the rates of birth defects, the occurrence of intrauterine growth retardation, fetal death, maternal bleeding, and infection. The risk of premature delivery and the rate of cesarean section in women who have undergone CVS also remain unknown.

Many doctors are now using CVS and promoting it as simple and safe. Until these and other long- and short-term risks to women are more fully explored, women must carefully consider all of their options by talking to a genetic counselor as well as to the doctor who will be doing the procedure. Ask about the reports that associate CVS with disabilities. Is the practitioner aware of the controversy about which part of the chorion should be sampled? Does s/he downplay other researchers' questions and conclusions because they do not fit into her/his own model of care?

You now know what the CVS process is. Before you choose to have or decline the procedure, read Book Three (p. 149), "To Test or Not to Test."

The following self-awareness exercise is meant only to help you clarify for yourself why you are considering the test.

The Choice for CVS

A. Check your reasons for considering CVS.

 ☐ It will reduce the waiting period.

 ☐ It will give me more privacy since my pregnancy is not yet obvious.

 ☐ It will allow me to have an earlier and safer abortion if a disability is discovered.

 ☐ I will be less stressed having this information earlier in my pregnancy.

B. Write down any other reasons.

_____

_____

_____

The Choice Against CVS

A. Check your reasons for not wanting CVS.

 ☐ It's still experimental.

 ☐ I don't want to be part of a research study.

 ☐ I can wait for amniocentesis at sixteen weeks.

 ☐ The fetal-loss rate is too high.

 ☐ It has too many unknowns, some of which are too risky.

 ☐ It will not tell me anything about neural tube disorders, whereas amniocentesis can tell me about chromosomes and neural tube defects.

 ☐ I don't want to apply any technology to this pregnancy experience.

B. Write down any other reasons.

_____

_____

_____

Now that you have clarified your own thinking about CVS, discuss it with your partner and your health care provider. Then consult Book Three (p. 145) for help in choosing or refusing this test.

8 | Percutaneous Umbilical Blood Sampling (PUBS) and Other Prenatal Tests

It is likely that the entire world of prenatal testing will have changed by the year 2000 if the pace of research and discoveries keeps up with that of the past twenty years. Medical schools, genetic laboratories, and large corporations are all exploring new techniques. Their motives, their promises, and their technology will need careful scrutiny so that we can evaluate both the benefits and the risks of what they have to offer.

To study the genetic blueprint of a fetus, the fetal cells, tissue, or blood must be examined. Presently, amniocentesis and chorionic villus sampling are the methods available for obtaining direct fetal components, but new tests are being developed and added to the prenatal genetic testing package.

WHAT IS PUBS?

PUBS is one of the newest experimental methods of fetal blood sampling. Fetal blood is obtained by guiding a needle through the abdomen and uterus into the umbilical vein.

The umbilical cord contains blood vessels (two arteries and one vein) that connect the woman and fetus. The vein brings blood from the placenta to the fetus. The arteries take blood from the fetus to the placenta. Since there is no direct connection between the fetal blood and the woman's blood, in theory this test allows direct measurement of the fetal blood components. It is used to assess fetal health.

USES OF PUBS

PUBS can be used to test for many of the same genetic conditions as is amniocentesis (see p. 75). It is used for 1) chromosome studies to identify conditions such as Down syndrome; 2) fluid analysis to identify substances indicative of spina bifida; 3) biochemical studies to look for conditions that affect metabolism, such as Tay-Sachs disease; 4) DNA studies to look for conditions that have a specific pattern of inheritance, such as cystic fibrosis, sickle-cell anemia, or Duchenne muscular dystrophy; 5) determining whether the fetus is male or female. In addition, this test can be used to look for the presence of certain antibodies to fetal infections, such as rubella, toxoplasmosis, or AIDS. Because it provides a direct connection to the fetus, it can also be used to provide intrauterine blood transfusions, medications, such as cardiac antiarrhythmics or hormones, and, eventually, to replace missing enzymes or proteins.

PUBS FOR WHOM?

Although PUBS can provide information similar to amniocentesis and can be done for the same women who are candidates for amniocentesis, it is currently being offered only under special circumstances. Your doctor may offer this test to you if the following conditions exist:

1) You decide late in your pregnancy to begin prenatal testing and want a fast result.

2) It is late in your pregnancy and an abnormality has been noted on ultrasound.

3) Your practitioner considers it more accurate than amniocentesis or is involved in research with PUBS.

4) Amniocentesis results are not conclusive and you want to confirm the results.

5) You have been exposed to an infectious disease that could potentially affect fetal development.

6) There is a need to measure a drug or chemical level in the fetal blood.

7) There is a blood incompatibility (Rh disease).

TIMING THE TEST

Although experience with PUBS is limited, it is being performed between eighteen and thirty-six weeks of pregnancy. Before eighteen weeks the blood vessels are too fragile and do not stay still. After twenty-four weeks the test may be offered even though pregnancy termination may no longer be an option.

COSTS OF PUBS

The costs of PUBS varies between $500 and $800. Because PUBS is still experimental, not all insurance companies cover the cost of this procedure.

WHERE TO GO FOR PUBS

Currently, PUBS is performed in a hospital setting, where there is immediate medical backup should a complication of the test arise. Most doctors refer pregnant women to a research center where an obstetrician who has had extensive training in PUBS will perform the test. An experienced ultrasonographer should also be part of the team. Before you make your decision to have the PUBS test, ask the doctor how many PUBS procedures s/he performs per week, per month, or per year. Since an experienced laboratory is almost as important as an experienced doctor, ask your health care provider where the fetal blood sample will be analyzed.

INFORMED CONSENT

If you decide to have this test, you will be asked to sign a form stating that you understand that the procedure is still experimental and that you agree to it.

BEFORE PUBS

If you choose to have the PUBS procedure, you will be asked for information on your blood type. If you are Rh-negative and your baby's father is Rh-positive, an injection of immune globulin will be recommended.

PREPARATION FOR PUBS

For many women the thought of a needle entering their womb causes great concern and anxiety. A normal response to this type of stress is to tighten or contract the abdominal muscles. This reflex can cause further physical and emotional tension. If you do choose to have PUBS, prepare yourself by practicing relaxation techniques to use during the procedure.

You may want to ask your partner to be with you during the

actual PUBS procedure to provide moral support and physical comfort for you. This type of involvement and presence will help you feel that your pregnancy is a shared experience. Obviously, invite your partner to be with you only if that will make you feel more calm.

PRE-PUBS ULTRASOUND

A diagnostic ultrasound (p. 60) should always be done just before you have the PUBS test. The pre-PUBS ultrasound will accurately assess the age of your baby, establish if you are carrying more than one baby, assess the shape and position of your uterus and the umbilical cord, rule out any abnormality that could cause a complication of the procedure, and determine where to insert the needle.

The ultrasound will be kept on during the entire PUBS procedure so that the position of the placenta, fetus, and umbilical cord are visible during the needle insertion.

THE PUBS PROCEDURE

If you choose to have PUBS, you will be asked to lie flat on your back on a narrow table. You will have to expose your abdomen, so it is best to wear a shirt and slacks rather than a dress. Your doctor, wearing sterile gloves, will put a sterile sheet above and below your abdomen. S/he will then clean your abdominal area with a cold, wet antiseptic solution. Sometimes a local anesthetic, such as Xylocaine, will be injected near the place of the needle insertion.

Once your abdomen is "prepped," the doctor will pass a needle through your abdomen, through your uterine muscle, through the amniotic sac, and into the umbilical vein. This needle is longer than the one used for amniocentesis. A syringe is then attached to the needle and a small amount of fetal blood is withdrawn. If the PUBS test is unsuccessful after two attempts, you should consider whether or not to repeat the test.

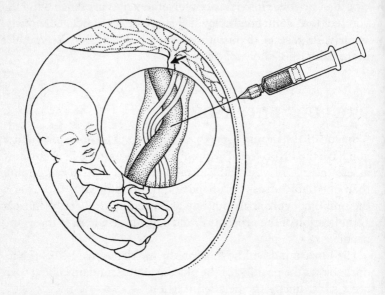

AFTER THE PUBS

After the PUBS test, your baby's heart movements should be carefully observed on the ultrasound machine. Your doctor will probably give you specific instructions on such matters as activity, exercise, and lovemaking. If s/he does not, ask what precautions are appropriate. Although many physicians do not think that any change in schedule is necessary after the PUBS procedure, some women will naturally want to rest. This can contribute to your general physical and emotional well-being.

After the procedure you should be on the lookout for any rise in your temperature or any leakage of amniotic fluid or blood either abdominally where the needle was inserted or vaginally.

RECEIVING PUBS RESULTS

Because blood is a living tissue, analyzing fetal blood in the laboratory produces a faster chromosome analysis than amniocentesis. Amniocentesis requires ten to fourteen days for cells to grow whereas PUBS can theoretically generate results in three days.

Ask your health care provider how you will be notified about your PUBS results. If your provider sends the blood to an outside laboratory, the laboratory should notify your provider immediately of all abnormal test results. If you feel anxious during the waiting period, request that you be notified immediately by phone with the test results, whether they are normal or abnormal.

NORMAL PUBS RESULTS

In order to interpret a normal result, you should know what conditions or substances are being tested for. A normal result usually means that your baby has the proper size, shape, and number of chromosomes (twenty-two pairs or forty-four auto-somes) and two gender-related chromosomes (either XX for female or XY for male). This means the baby probably does not have a chromosome variation. If the amniotic fluid substances are normal, it means the baby probably does not have an open neural tube condition, like spina bifida.

NORMAL VARIATIONS

A number of fetal chromosomal variations have not been associated with any clinical effects in the fetus. For example, certain inversions on a chromosome (INV9), dark stains in certain places of one chromosome (QHPLUS), or extra material on a Y chromosome (XYQHPLUS) may be normal variants and not significant. This is another anxiety-provoking situation that you may want to be prepared for if you have the PUBS test.

ABNORMAL RESULTS

In the rare instance that an abnormal finding is identified, you will be told that your fetus has whatever condition is indicated.

PUBS can be testing for variations in chromosomes, biochemical or metabolic substances, changes in DNA, drug levels, or antibodies to fetal infections. You could be told that the test reveals a chromosome condition such as Down syndrome, a biochemical variation such as spina bifida, a metabolic deficiency such as Tay-Sachs, a blood disorder such as sickle-cell anemia, or the presence of antibodies to toxoplasmosis. Bear in mind that the fluid may not have been analyzed for all these potential conditions. Your results will only be as complete as the test.

Because the PUBS test is not always perfect, you need to understand that a baby can be born with a disability after a "normal" PUBS. There is also the chance that a healthy baby may be incorrectly identified as having a disability. Whatever the "abnormal" results, you should not be pushed into an immediate decision. Think carefully about the implications of the results.

When PUBS is offered in the third trimester, you will not have the option to terminate your pregnancy if a condition is discovered. For that reason, before submitting to the test you should consider what you want to know and when. Some women who unexpectedly do learn in the third trimester that their baby has a disability are given anti-anxiety drugs to help them cope with the information. Others use the information to help them prepare for the delivery and possible care of their baby after birth. Other women have said that they would rather not have known until the birth that their baby had a disabling condition.

If you choose to have this test and a disability is found, discuss the details of the birthing process with your health care provider. It may be that you will want to have surgical and social support nearby. For example, if you learn that your fetus has spina bifida, you may decide to have a cesarean section, since it is now believed that this type of birth produces less stress on the fetal nervous system and possibly fewer complications of the condition.

Some women whose fetuses have a disability may not want interventions used during the birth. The information can be used to prepare for how the baby will be treated once it is born—whether you want heroic measures, such as routine life-saving devices used, or whether you want to allow nature to take its course. If you choose to have this test, these are details to talk about with your health care provider and with someone in the neonatal intensive care unit (NICU) where your baby may be placed after it is born if a disability is identified.

ACCURACY OF PUBS

Although there has been limited experience with PUBS, laboratory analysis of fetal blood is considered highly accurate. Since this particular test is so new, there are numerous factors still being explored. For example, concerns about which part of the umbilical cord should be sampled are still being debated. The current thinking is that, in order to produce reliable results, inserting the needle into the umbilical cord at the placental site is the best technique. Obviously the accuracy of results is dependent on the tests performed on the sample. If the specimen is being analyzed for the presence of antibodies to indicate whether the fetus has been exposed to a certain infection, the accuracy of the results is dependent on the sensitivity of the antibody test itself. As with amniocentesis, there are other problems that can occur in the laboratory that might affect your results (see p. 87).

RISKS OF PUBS

Obtaining a fetal blood sample is not a simple technique. The diameter of the umbilical cord is relatively small. Since the baby is in motion *in utero,* the umbilical cord is often moving within the amniotic fluid. Stabilizing it in order to insert a needle is an extremely difficult feat because when the baby moves, the cord can move, too, and throw the needle off target. The pressure of the needle at the moment of puncture can also cause the fetus to move and can dislodge the needle tip while the sample is being aspirated. When the needle is pulled out, blood can be mixed with the amniotic fluid and the sample may become useless. If repeated insertions are needed, a woman must decide whether the benefits of the procedure outweigh the risks.

The assertion that PUBS is safe enough to offer pregnant women is based on limited experience and minimizes the possible complications that can and do occur. The risks for a woman and for the fetus are similar to those of amniocentesis: infection, bleeding, isoimmunization, harm to the fetus, and miscarriage at an estimated rate of 1 to 2 percent. There are also several other risks that are particular to PUBS. These include perforation of the uterine arteries, clotting in the fetal cord, and premature delivery. The long-term effects, if any, are unknown. Since the total blood volume of the fetus is small, withdrawing any fetal blood must be done with extreme care and caution.

You now know what the PUBS test is. Before you choose to have or decline the procedure, read Book Three (p. 149), "To Test or Not to Test."

OTHER PRENATAL TESTS

Fetoscopy

Fetoscopy is an experimental surgical procedure that entails inserting a fetoscope (a thin telescope-like instrument with a fiberoptic lens) through the abdomen into the uterus. This procedure gives the obstetrician a narrow-angle view of the amniotic fluid, the placenta, and isolated parts of the fetus.

At present, fetoscopy is used only when specific problems are suspected. It is used to confirm results from a prior procedure or to assess the severity of a disability already identified (i.e., cleft lip or a missing limb seen on ultrasound). It has been used in conjunction with other fetal blood sampling techniques. In addition, it can be used to determine the prospects for performing fetal surgery *in utero*.

A woman prepares for fetoscopy much like she would for the PUBS test. It is done under ultrasound guidance (see p. 60). The doctor determines the location of the fetus, placenta, and umbilical cord, and then may inject a local anesthetic into the abdomen. An incision is made and a cannula is pushed down through the abdomen and passed through the uterus directly into the amniotic sac. The doctor then inserts the fetoscope through the cannula in order to see the fetus. This procedure is performed during the fifteenth to eighteenth week of pregnancy if the purpose is to look at fetal anatomy. (At this point the amniotic fluid is clear and the fetus is small enough that it can be seen adequately.)

In order to make a reliable examination and interpretation from fetoscopy, a doctor needs to recognize normal fetal development and understand the genetics and variability of a condition. Fetoscopy can result in the same kind of complications that arise with amniocentesis, but there is a higher risk of fetal loss. Because of its complexity, fetoscopy is, as of this writing, performed only in a few medical research centers by obstetricians (fetoscoptists) who have had extensive training.

Cell Sorting

Researchers have known for some time that from at least the second month of pregnancy, small amounts of fetal cells "leak" into a pregnant woman's circulatory system. A few research centers are experimenting with new laser technology to isolate fetal cells from a pregnant woman's blood. If pure fetal cells can be obtained, researchers hope to use the cells to perform genetic screening and diagnostic tests. The development of this type of technology is eventually expected to make invasive procedures like amniocentesis or CVS obsolete.

Fetal Skin Sampling

Some researchers are experimenting with fetal tissue sampling or "skin biopsy" to diagnose several rare hereditary skin disorders. Skin tissue can be used in genetic diagnosis because the skin cells multiply quickly and contain genetic information. It is also becoming possible to use fetal skin fragments to measure drug concentration levels or possible teratogens from the environment that reach the fetus. Fetal tissue sampling is done under fetoscopy. Researchers claim that the sample of fetal tissue that is obtained from the scalp, buttocks, or trunk leaves no noticeable scar. There is really not enough evidence yet to know the risks, accuracy, and long-term effects of this type of procedure.

DNA-Based Tests (Gene Probe Tests)

DNA-based tests are among the newest experimental laboratory tests that screen for genetic conditions. DNA testing is used to identify the presence or absence of markers indicative of single-gene conditions, such as cystic fibrosis, Duchenne muscular dystrophy, Huntington disease, and hemophilia, that, up until recently, could not be identified prenatally.

DNA testing is known as a "family test," or "linkage test," because it often requires a number of family members to have their genetic material analyzed before a disability can be confirmed in the fetus. It's usually recommended that families with a history of one of these conditions have DNA-based tests before prenatal testing if not prior to pregnancy.

The test's accuracy depends on the condition being tested for, whether the gene has been identified to a specific location on a chromosome, and the type of probes being used to track the presence of the gene. For example, with Duchenne muscular dystrophy, the exact location of the gene that causes the condition is still unknown. Therefore, the presence of a disease-causing gene can only be inferred from complicated studies. With other conditions, such as sickle-cell anemia or thalassemia, the variant gene can be identified directly in the adult or fetus, and family studies are not required.

Accuracy is also dependent on the type of fetal sample being used. Chorionic villi are considered the "specimen of choice" since adequate amounts of DNA can be directly prepared from the tissue. Although amniocentesis is more common than CVS, the amniotic fluid cells need to be grown in the laboratory to provide enough of a sample for DNA testing. Fetal blood sampling may not provide enough DNA for these studies.

The results of DNA linkage testing are given in terms of "informativeness." "Fully informative" means there is enough genetic material to track the relevant chromosome. "Partially informative" means only incomplete information can be obtained. "Uninformative" means that it is impossible to say what the probability is that a fetus or adult has the disability-causing gene.

Although most of the work on this experimental technology occurs in research laboratories, a transition is being made to clinical practice. Many commercial laboratories and a number of university medical laboratories offer DNA-based services on a fee-for-service basis. A family of four may be evaluated for a fee ranging from $400 to $600. Other family members who require testing (this may include the fetus) are generally charged an additional fee of approximately $200 dollars.

Because of the experimental nature of these rapidly changing tests, their psychological implications, and the need for accurate counseling in using the results, individuals considering them should speak with knowledgeable professionals. Currently, there is minimal external regulation of DNA tests and other laboratory procedures. Guidelines for these tests are only now being formulated.

Over-the-Counter Tests

Tests to determine the sex of your baby are available in drugstores and by mail for home use. No one knows anything much about their accuracy and it is advised that you do not rely upon their results.

As genetic screening becomes more refined, test kits to screen for fetal disabilities, such as Down syndrome or spina bifida, may be available for use at home. The potential for decision-making about what we choose to know and not to know may eventually shift from the doctor's office to the drugstore.

Prenatal Tests in Late Pregnancy

One of the most common reasons for intervention in late pregnancy is that the baby is overdue (after forty weeks). The causes of prolonged pregnancy remain a mystery. Sometimes a woman is perceived as overdue because of an error in calculating the due date; some women simply appear to take longer for the gestation period. There may be other hormonal and psychological explanations.

Some practitioners consider an overdue baby as a natural occurrence which they need to watch. Others are more concerned about the potential risks to the fetus. Recommendations for what to do when a baby is late often depend on the philosophy of the provider. Two commonly used tests in this situation are the nonstress and the contraction stress tests, both based on fetal heart rate monitoring by Doppler ultrasound. When there is concern, pregnancy may be induced.

A blood or urine sample may be taken to measure the amount of the hormone estriol in the woman's body as an indication of possible fetal distress. Samples of amniotic fluid also may be taken through amniocentesis to measure certain compounds that may indicate lung maturity.

Tests in Labor

During labor itself, especially if you are delivering in a hospital, you will probably be hooked up to an external fetal monitor. A belt-like device may be placed on your abdomen to monitor fetal heart movement by ultrasound and to record uterine contractions. The information received will be printed out on a strip of paper, much like an electrocardiogram. Many women find that the use of the monitor restricts their movements in a way that makes them very uncomfortable. It's also important to remember that the interpretation of these data very much depends on the experience and attitude of the person reading them. False interpretations have been incorrectly noted.

Internal fetal monitoring involves rupturing the membranes (bag of water). A fluid-filled plastic tube is inserted through the vagina into the uterus alongside the fetus. Changes in pressure are transmitted and recorded through a monitoring machine. In order to assess fetal health, an electrode with a spiral end is inserted into the baby's scalp. The resultant information is monitored to see whether there is fetal distress, to measure the level of oxygen, etc.

The risks of external fetal monitoring have not been fully assessed. More is known about the risks of internal fetal monitoring. Infection may occur as a result of the frequent vaginal examinations and manipulation, the rupturing of the membranes, or the insertion of the electrode. The fetus may experience infection because its skin has been punctured. Another, more subtle concern, is whether too many unnecessary cesarean sections are being performed as a result of misinterpretation of fetal heart rate monitoring or overreaction to the data. Electronic fetal monitoring may offer benefits to high-risk pregnancies, but the benefits to normal pregnancies are questionable.

9 | If a Test Result Is Abnormal . . .

The most difficult part of prenatal testing is thinking about what you would do if you were told your baby has a disability. Even if you learn as much as possible about the individual tests, you may resist thinking about your options. Most women who have prenatal testing avoid "what if" conversations. They say, "If the results are abnormal . . . I'll cross that bridge when I come to it," or, "Why think about 'the worst' scenario now? Everything will be fine." Nevertheless, if you are considering prenatal testing, it is wise to think about how you might feel if you were to receive an abnormal test result.

FEELINGS

It is natural to want the best for your child, including good health. Just as there is no good way, whatever the skills of your doctor, to tell people their fetus may be disabled, there is no way to predict how you would feel if you got that news. You may realize that "accidents can happen," but you say to yourself, "not to me," "not to my baby." Try to imagine how you might feel or what you might do if you were told, "There is something wrong with your baby." How would you react if you were told that your fetus had a correctable heart condition? What if you were told that your fetus had Down syndrome? Cleft lip? A missing finger? How might you feel? What questions would you want to ask? What information would you need to know before you could make a decision about what to do? What conditions, if any, would you find acceptable?

Some women who are told their fetus has a disability are just grateful to have a baby—even with the attendant problems. They trust and hope for the best. Other women experience feelings of sadness, anger, and loneliness. They may begin to mourn the loss of the normal baby they expected. They may be in shock or not believe the test results or feel that people are holding back information. They may also feel anger toward the doctor who made the diagnosis for being the "bearer of bad news." Or they may be angry with themselves, their partner, their fetus, or their other children. Some women say they feel hatred toward the "baby" itself and a sense of shame and revulsion at the idea of carrying a disabled fetus in their womb. Other women feel a mixture of love, sadness, and hurt for their baby. These feelings might conflict with one another. This is understandable.

Feelings are neither right or wrong, positive or negative. Feelings take time to work through, and that process can help you understand what you want to do.

Many women who learn that their fetus has a disability ask, "Why is this happening to me?" They have learned their response to prenatal-testing results within a social context: they are surrounded by books, magazines, and pamphlets telling them "How to Have the Healthiest Baby You Can," "Be Good to Your Baby Before It Is Born," "Think Before You Drink," "Stop Smoking for Your Baby's Sake," etc. Therefore, they ask, "Is it that glass of wine I drank, the medicine I took for morning sickness, the pot I smoked when I was younger? Or is this God's way of punishing me for what I'm doing wrong?" It is hard to accept the thought that usually we are not responsible for the occurrence of disabilities in our unborn. As we've seen, many, many factors come into play, most of them out of our control.

VISIONS OF DISABILITY

For each of us, "disability" calls forth particular images and reactions, some of them frightening. What kinds of images does it evoke? Do you imagine suffering? Or do you envision a special child who may enrich your life and that of others? Which of your joys and hopes in having a child would be changed if s/he had a disability? Women have told me that their imagined fears of a baby with a disability have frequently caused them more distress than the baby's actual disability.

The way the disability is presented to you will also influence your attitude about your options. Some doctors and genetic counselors describe disabilities in ways that cause apprehension. For example, a physician may use the word *gross* when s/he means "big," but the slang interpretation makes you think "ugly." Talking about a fetus as "defective," "a handicapped victim," or a "pathetic case" are other examples of the way words can make us think about disabilities. Such negative images have been woven into the fabric of our society and greatly influence our feelings.

ACCESS TO INFORMATION ABOUT DISABILITIES

Before you can decide what to do if you receive an abnormal prenatal test result, you need accurate and relevant information about the particular disability. Many obstetricians do not have sophisticated information about disabilities, and much of the available literature is unrealistically discouraging. Predictions for life-span and extent of functional disabilities can be inaccurate and depressing.

For example, one woman learned through prenatal testing that her baby had spina bifida. She was told that the baby would never walk and would be mentally retarded. This woman chose to have the baby anyway. After a surgical operation at birth to correct the spinal disorder, her baby was left with only a scar and a slight limp. She is of normal intelligence.

Another woman learned through prenatal testing that her baby had Down syndrome. All she was told was that the child would be mentally retarded. This conjured up numerous images and stereotypes of a child who might need to be institutionalized. She was not told that there is a wide variation in intellectual abilities and that though some people with Down syndrome are seriously retarded, others are only mildly so. Neither was she told that early intervention and stimulation, special education, and a loving family can enhance the life of such a child. Many children with Down syndrome read, write, take music lessons, play sports, play with friends, go to summer camp, and have a job and, as adults, pay taxes.

It is impossible to predict what the life of your fetus will be like based on prenatal testing. Most disabilities are variable and will be expressed in different ways. Obviously the decision you make may be influenced by the type and severity of the disability. Women who have received abnormal prenatal diagnoses have found that talking with other parents of similarly disabled children can be helpful. Although each child is unique, knowing the potential range of what life can be like for the disabled child and the family can help you decide.

If you do not know such a family, or your provider can't assist you, you may want to get in touch with one of the organizations or parent-support groups listed in the appendix (see pp. 226–245). Counselors with training in genetics and prenatal testing may be able to help you deal with your concerns. There are also organizations that are advocates for the physically challenged that can be helpful (pp. 226–245).

YOUR OWN SUPPORT SYSTEM

Your feelings about confirmed abnormal testing results will also be influenced by your circumstances at the time. The kind of social, moral, and economic support that you have may be essential elements in how you decide to act on prenatal testing results. For example, is your partner going to support your choice? Do you have the necessary insurance? Can the place you live in be adapted to the special needs of a disabled child?

YOUR OPTIONS IF YOU RECEIVE ABNORMAL TEST RESULTS

This chapter and the next one describe the options available to women who learn their baby has a disability. Among the options you might consider are to:

continue your pregnancy, give birth to your baby, and keep him/her.

continue your pregnancy and let nature take its course, understanding your baby may die after birth.

continue your pregnancy, give birth, and offer your baby for adoption.

have fetal surgery *in utero* (if available).

have an abortion. (See following chapter, p. 134.)

It is important to realize that there is no right or wrong option for dealing with abnormal prenatal testing results. The hardest part may be deciding which choice feels right for you. But if you think about your options before you make the decision to test, you will be more prepared for any unexpected outcomes. As you read on about the options available to you, keep in mind the following questions:

- If medical treatment is available for a disability (*in utero* or after birth), would that influence your decision?

- Do you have a supportive partner, relatives, or close friends who can help with this decision?

- Do you have the financial resources you may need if you choose a specific option?

- Are there special services and programs in your area that might be helpful if you were to make a certain choice?

- Are you ready to deal with the consequences of your choice, whatever it may be?

- Which option or decision will make you feel the best now? In the future? Are there several options you are considering?

ABNORMAL TESTING RESULTS AND YOUR OPTIONS

Continue Your Pregnancy, Give Birth to Your Baby, and Keep Her/Him

Becoming a parent changes your life forever. You will have new demands on your time and you will be responsible for the care and development of a new person. Because all children are unique, it's impossible to generalize about what life is like raising a disabled child, and whether it is more difficult than, say, a very demanding able-bodied child.

If you learn that your fetus has a disability, you need to decide about continuing or terminating your pregnancy. Many women choose to continue their pregnancy and to raise their disabled child. Some even adopt other disabled children.

When thinking about parenting a disabled child, consider how you will care for your child and do all the other things you want to do. How might the disability affect your child when s/he grows up? How will other family members deal with the special needs or situations? One woman said that her biggest problem in raising a disabled child was the obstacles other people put in her way. Another woman said, "If you are accepting and loving toward your baby who is disabled, others will know how they should act. They will follow your example." Some parents talk of terrible suffering they experience in trying to raise children with disabilities; others seem to achieve personal growth as a result of raising a child with special needs.

Though eligibility requirements vary, most states provide some services to families who have a child with a disability. These may include home and respite care, public health nurses, counseling, medical services, financial services, and special education programs. Extended living or day-care programs and institutional care may also be available. To find out more about your state services, get in touch with your state genetics program listed in the appendix (see pp. 246–251).

Continue Your Pregnancy, Understanding Your Baby May Die After Birth

What if you learn that your fetus has a disability which, if untreated after birth, might result in death? For women who do not want to have an abortion, "letting nature run its course" may be an option. However, the results of recent lawsuits could interfere in this plan in that they require hospitals to prolong as long as possible the lives of newborns with handicaps.

Recently, for example, a woman learned through prenatal testing that her fetus had anencephaly (no brain). The longest a newborn with this condition has survived is a few weeks. This woman continued her pregnancy and arranged to donate the baby's organs when s/he ceased to live. Organ donation is only practical in the presence of certain disabilities and certainly should not be considered if the idea adds to your feelings of stress.

Adoption

If you were to learn that your fetus has a disability and you don't feel prepared to handle raising the infant after birth, adoption is an option. There are people who want to adopt infants with special physical and emotional needs.

If you were to "surrender" your baby, a number of licensed adoption agencies will let you specify the type of family and home you would like to see the baby live in. Some agencies use a process in which you receive letters from couples who want your child, and you then select among them the parents you want for your baby. Potential adoptive parents have even been known to attend the birth of the child. There are also new legal "open adoption" arrangements that allow visitation or continued contact between families if that is what you want.

Many women who have given up their disabled child for adoption have done so out of love and the belief that the adoptive parents could offer emotional and physical comfort that they could not provide. Adoption may be seen as the only alternative for women who feel they do not want an abortion.

For some women, carrying a disabled fetus to term and then giving up the infant for adoption seems more agonizing than having an abortion. The idea that someone else could be more capable of raising their child may be painful and embarrassing. How do you feel about adoption as an option? How would you feel about the idea of someone else raising your child if a disability is present? Would you rather terminate your pregnancy than deal with the implications posed by adoption? Adoption can be a loving act but the decision must be based on scrupulous self-questioning. To find out more about adoption, talk with your provider or contact a special needs adoption agency.

Fetal Therapies *in Utero*

Several experimental medical and surgical therapies are being used to correct conditions *in utero* before the fetus sustains permanent harm that may not be correctable after birth.

Prenatal surgery on the fetus is in its pioneer stages, although developing rapidly. Thus far, some surgery has successfully corrected problems, while other operations have been of questionable value.

Obstructive hydrocephalus, "water on the brain," has been treated prenatally by repeatedly withdrawing fluid from the fetal brain or with the use of tubes that are placed in the fetal head to drain into the amniotic fluid. Excess fluid in the fetal lungs and certain kidney conditions have also been alleviated by fetal surgery. There have even been operations that have involved removing the fetus from the womb, performing surgery on it, then returning it to the uterus. Surgical research on fetal sheep and primates suggests that hernias, certain stomach conditions, and spina bifida are potential conditions for fetal surgery in humans.

In addition to surgery, drugs are being prescribed to treat certain conditions detected prenatally. A prime example is utilizing Rhogam in the presence of Rh disease. Steroids are given to pregnant women prior to an early delivery in order to enhance fetal lung maturity. Thyroxine (a hormone) can be injected directly into fetuses with hypothyroidism. Digitalis, a cardiac medication, is administered when fetal cardiac arrhythmias are identified. Vitamin therapy and folic-acid replacements are also being prescribed for certain conditions. New human gene therapies such as direct enzyme replacement, bone-marrow transplantation, and gene transfers remain in preliminary stages of development.

Although the future is uncertain, there has been an increase in funds for fetal research. While fetal surgery and human gene therapies have the potential of broadening our options, if certain disabilities are found, neither is a trivial procedure. If we allow the fetus to become the patient, we soon may have no choice regarding these types of procedures.

If fetal treatments, either medical or surgical, would be an alternative for you, you have many issues to consider. Of major importance is knowing what risk the procedure is to your own health. Find out what the success rate is for the procedure, the dangers to the unborn child, and how many times this particular surgeon has performed this particular procedure. There are only a few centers around the world that treat the fetus. Obviously, if this would be an option for you, you would need to learn a new body of medical information and approach it cautiously.

10

Abnormal Test Results and Abortion

If you learn that your fetus has a disability and you consider abortion, you will be among the women who have the experience of carrying a once-wanted child that you suddenly choose not to bear. For some women, terminating a pregnancy in the presence of a disability provides a sense of relief. They feel grateful that they do not have to have the responsibility of parenting a disabled child. They may, at the same time, feel a sense of loss. Some women begin to mourn the baby they expected. They may feel angry, helpless, or depressed. Choosing abortion, like the other options, can put stress on relationships with a partner, friends, or family.

Before making a decision about abortion, you may want to discuss the results of your prenatal diagnostic evaluation and the disability with your partner, with someone who has had an abortion, a genetic counselor, your doctor, a geneticist, and perhaps with a parent organization that is an advocacy group for the specific disability (see p. 226). Or you may not want to talk with anyone.

Acknowledge and deal with your feelings of relief or sadness, your reactions of anger or confusion, and your concerns. Try to avoid tranquilizers or antidepressant drugs that might suppress or postpone the grief, because these may actually prolong the natural course of grieving. Remember, don't feel pressured by someone else's decision or choice. You will be facing a decision whose consequences you will have to bear. You will weigh the information you receive, your own life situation, and your ethical beliefs in deciding whether or not to have an abortion. But it's a hard decision that, finally, only you can make.

METHODS OF ABORTION

Many different types of abortions are performed in the United States. Each procedure has its own limitations and benefits, but the primary way to avoid complications is to have the abortion performed by an experienced doctor. In general, the earlier the abortion, the safer it is. The type of operation will depend on the age and size of your fetus and the laws of your state.

It is important to know about the different methods of abortion because not all techniques are practiced by all professionals. If you are confronted with this decision, discuss the options with your health care provider to see whether s/he is skilled in performing the type of abortion you might consider, and whether it is applicable to your situation.

PRE-ABORTION COUNSELING

If you choose to have an abortion because your fetus has a disability, speak with a preabortion counselor about your decision. Ask for a step-by-step description of the procedure, its risks and possible complications, and what you might expect physically and emotionally after the procedure. During counseling, also ask for full information about anesthesia—its uses, limitations, and risks. Some women, for example, have used acupuncture or other homeopathic pain relievers to diminish pain before, during, and after an abortion. Before an abortion procedure, a woman is usually asked to sign an informed consent form that indicates that she is fully aware of all components of the operation.

PREPARING FOR AN ABORTION

A woman choosing to terminate her pregnancy needs access to well-qualified doctors and counselors. In order to find the right person and place, call a local women's health center or ask your health care provider for a list of safe and qualified personnel and facilities.

If you were to have a first-trimester abortion and if you do not have any specific medical condition that makes a hospital abortion advisable (such as a serious heart or lung condition, uncontrolled epilepsy, diabetes, or a bleeding disorder), you may want to go to an abortion clinic or have the procedure in your doctor's office. Hospital-based abortion protocols sometimes involve wide dilation of the cervical opening rather than the lesser dilatation using the small, safe, flexible cannulas. Whether you're going to a private doctor, a clinic, or a hospital, make sure the practitioner is well trained and experienced.

Since most abortions for fetal disabilities still occur in the second trimester, many women who choose to abort will be hospitalized (although some physicians will do outpatient office abortions until twenty-two weeks). Plan to have the abortion in a center whose staff will offer its full support. Try to have your partner present during the actual procedure and remain with you throughout your recovery period.

The attitudes and behavior of the health care personnel involved in your care around the time of an abortion are extremely important. Some doctors and nurses may find it difficult to support a woman, either because of religious beliefs or because, as medical professionals trained to treat, cure, and even prolong "life," they may find it hard to accept abortion. Unless the practitioners involved in your care are specifically trained in supporting women through the abortion process, you may encounter people with personal biases against your course of action.

FIRST-TRIMESTER ABORTION PROCEDURES

During the first trimester, dilatation and evacuation (D&E), otherwise known as vacuum aspiration, and dilatation and curettage (D&C) are used. These first-trimester procedures are usually performed in an outpatient facility. A woman who has had chorionic villus sampling (CVS) in the first trimester and who chooses to terminate her pregnancy could select one of these procedures. (Abortion herbs have also been used by some women in early pregnancy. This practice is ancient, but there has been little research to evaluate its effects. Some herbs appear safe, while others are very dangerous, particularly in large doses.)

Dilatation and Evacuation (D&E)

For a D&E, a woman is told not to eat for three to four hours prior to the procedure. This is to avoid any vomiting or aspiration. The doctor, usually a trained gynecologist, will ask you to lie on an examining table and to put your feet into stirrups (the lithotomy position). A speculum will be inserted into your vagina and opened. Some women experience this as an uncomfortable feeling of pressure. The doctor will then perform a vaginal pelvic examination to check the angle of your uterus and measure its depth.

If you have local anesthesia, a novocaine-like substance, will be injected along the nerves of your cervix. The cervix is then dilated with metal rods, or probes, and a plastic tube attached to an aspiration machine is inserted into the uterus. Suction will be applied to remove the fetal tissue. The best abortion technique is that which uses as little dilatation as possible. The further along you are in your pregnancy, the larger the dilator may need to be.

Many women feel cramping during the dilatation part of the abortion. Deep breathing, creative visualizations, and other relaxation techniques may help to ease the discomfort.

Dilatation and Curettage

If you have a D&C, the preparatory method is similar to evacuation. However, instead of suction, the doctor scrapes the inner lining of the uterus with a curette.

Most first-trimester abortion procedures take about twenty minutes. The possible complications include infection, bleeding, hemorrhage, lacerations to the cervix, or perforation or tearing of the uterus. However, most abortions performed in the first trimester of pregnancy are safe.

DRUGS TO INDUCE ABORTION

A new medicine called RU486 (Mifepristone) is being developed as an alternative to a first-trimester surgical abortion. This synthetic medicine withdraws from the body progesterone, which is essential for maintaining a pregnancy. It causes the uterus to bleed and to expel the fetal contents. This experimental medicine is now used only in research studies with women who are six to eight weeks pregnant, and who are carrying an unwanted pregnancy. Researchers foresee, however, that it will soon be used in later weeks, possibly even after the CVS test. One study reported that RU486 was used to induce an abortion late in pregnancy when the baby had already died.

Complications of this drug treatment include prolonged bleeding and incomplete or failed abortion. No one knows exactly what the long-term effects of this medicine on a woman's body may be.

SECOND-TRIMESTER ABORTION PROCEDURES

A second-trimester abortion (fourteen to twenty-four weeks), also known as a therapeutic, selective, eugenic, or genetic abortion, may require that labor be induced by drugs to stimulate labor contractions and cause the fetus and placenta to be expelled through the vagina.

An abortion during the second trimester is usually performed in a hospital. You may or may not be required to stay overnight. This usually depends on how long the abortion takes and how you are feeling afterwards.

Dilatation and Evacuation

A D&E procedure (p. 137) can also be done in the second trimester, sometimes up until twenty-two weeks of pregnancy. But because second-trimester prenatal results are usually not confirmed until nineteen to twenty-one weeks, you may be too far along in your pregnancy for this type of procedure.

In the second trimester, general anesthesia may be used and, as an alternative to using metal rods to dilate the cervix, some doctors use a natural substance called *laminaria,* a compressed seaweed. Depending on how many weeks pregnant you are, one to six sticks of laminaria are inserted into your cervix the day before the abortion to dilate the opening. Laminaria works by gradually expanding as it absorbs the moisture from the cervix.

Prostaglandin Infusion

A prostaglandin infusion is probably the most commonly used abortion method for women who elect to terminate their pregnancy in the second trimester because of a fetal disability.

Prostaglandin, a natural substance contained in both semen and menstrual fluids, actually causes contractions of the uterus. With a prostaglandin abortion, synthetic prostaglandins are usually injected through your abdomen into the amniotic sac via amniocentesis. Contractions usually begin within a few hours. It can take up to twenty hours from the time of the injection before the abortion is completed.

The side effects of the prostaglandin injection are similar to those that can occur during a natural labor—nausea, vomiting, diarrhea, or sweating and chills. But they can also be serious. There have been reports of women having respiratory problems as a reaction to the prostaglandin. Hypertension, or high blood pressure, has also been known to occur.

Although it is rare, there have been situations in which a fetus was born breathing after a late second-trimester abortion that involves labor. This may have occurred because the fetal age was underestimated. Most providers require an ultrasound before second-trimester abortion. Generally, a fetus that has not reached twenty-eight weeks will not have lungs mature enough to survive. Depending on state law, when the fetus has "the capability of meaningful life outside the womb," the state may step in to regulate procedures and protect fetal life.

Saline Abortion

In saline abortions, used during the second trimester, some amniotic fluid is removed from the uterus via amniocentesis. Then a saline, or salt, solution is injected into the uterus. Within twelve to thirty-six hours, the contractions of labor begin, and both the fetus and the placenta are expelled vaginally.

A saline abortion is thought to be riskier than other types of abortion because absorption of high doses of salt can affect heart and kidney function. Since everyone's metabolism is different, it is also difficult to know what amount of saline should be injected.

The side effects of a saline abortion include headache, excessive thirst, high blood pressure, and possibly some alteration in consciousness. Saline abortions should not be performed on women who have preexisting hypertension or kidney or cardiac problems.

Hysterotomy

A hysterotomy is an abortion method that involves abdominal surgery. This procedure is much like a cesarean section, although the abdominal incision is smaller. You are given the choice of either general or spinal anesthesia, and an incision is made through the abdomen, the muscle layers, the uterus, and into the amniotic sac. Then the fetus and placenta are removed manually, and the incision is closed. This procedure is rarely used for abortion anymore because it carries all the risks of major surgery.

LONG-TERM EFFECTS OF ABORTION

Numerous studies have shown no increased risk of having a baby with a birth defect after having an abortion. The research does suggest however that a woman who has had *repeated* D&C abortions may have a greater chance of having a miscarriage, or a higher likelihood of having a baby born prematurely or with low birth weight, because of the weakening of the cervix that occurs with manipulation.

AFTER AN ABORTION

Some women find the psychological aftereffects of abortion very difficult; others do not. Talk to women who have been through the experience. You may, if possible, want to see the fetus. You may want to give the fetus a name, get its death certificate, or even hold burial or memorial services.

Some women have found such measures helpful. Others have decided that it's better not to give the aborted fetus so much reality and thus spare themselves what they consider needless pain.

FETOPSY/AUTOPSY

You may be asked to decide whether you want an autopsy, called a *fetopsy,* performed to determine the cause of your fetus's disability. Generally after an abortion or a miscarriage, the doctor will put the fetal tissue into a sterile container with a special solution to preserve the cells so that the fetus can be studied to determine if there were any genetic reasons for the disability. Some people want to know about the disability in their fetus. Was the cause genetic? Was it environmental? What are the chances of it occurring again? Can it be prevented?

There is a growing interest among doctors to study the fetus and a nationwide physicians' movement to obtain third-party reimbursement for this practice. An evaluation of a malformed fetus during fetopsy may include (1) a family history; (2) photographs to document the external features; (3) X rays; (4) chromosome analysis; (5) autopsy of fetal and placental tissue; and (6) blood slides. The hospital pathologists may do an examination of the fetus's body or send it to an outside laboratory for study. This procedure may take several weeks.

If you consent to a fetopsy, schedule an appointment to discuss the results with your health care provider, or ask for a copy of the pathology report. Your provider may help you decide whether or not other information or services, such as genetic counseling, might be useful to you before you plan another pregnancy.

DISCUSSING ABORTION WITH YOUR OTHER CHILDREN

Women often wonder how to tell their children about the health problems of their unborn baby, or of their decision to have an abortion.

The first step is to evaluate your children's understanding of the pregnancy, and then rehearse with a friend or relative what you are going to say to them. Consider including the following points:

1. No one is to blame for the baby's disability or death. Sometimes children think that because they wanted the unborn baby to "go away" they caused the problem. Many parents blame themselves and so it is no surprise that children may feel the same way.

2. No one else in the family is in danger of dying from the unborn baby's illness or disability. And you are not going to "get rid of" the existing children if they get sick or become disabled. If you choose to have an abortion, you may want to reemphasize that the unborn baby probably will not feel any pain and that you are doing what you feel is the best thing for yourself and your family. If you feel sad, allow your sadness to show—tears are a normal part of life. Your other children may even need to grieve with you.

Children have a marvelous capacity to understand and integrate. It may be better for them to know why you were feeling excited about the idea of a new baby at one point, and then feeling sad when you learned the baby has a problem, or that the baby will not be born. There are, however, children who may not want to know what's going on at all. If children in the family seem overly disturbed about the situation, you may want to seek professional help.

RELATIONSHIPS

Aborting a once-wanted baby because of a disability can cause difficulties in a relationship, especially if one of the partners is ambivalent about the abortion. Try to share your feelings; you may not grieve the same way. You may want to talk to other couples who have had this experience or to discuss the matter with a professional counselor.

If you are a single woman, your feelings will probably be like those of a married woman, but your need for support may be greater. Try to find another person to talk with who will recognize your special needs at this time.

REACTIONS OF RELATIVES AND FRIENDS

Because abortion is such a complicated issue, people will react differently to your decision. Some people will support and comfort you. Others may never mention the loss of your baby, and others may criticize you. One woman said that when she told her family about her plans for a funeral service for the fetus, she was told that "it wasn't necessary, not to make a fuss, and that it was morose." If someone does make a remark that hurts you, you can avoid an argument by saying something like, "I am making the best decision for myself at this time." Recognize that as others struggle with their own feelings, they might have difficulty relating to how you feel.

One way to handle the isolation that you may feel is to create a constellation of support people. If friends and relatives are unable to support your decision, get in touch with one of the organizations like Support for Prenatal Decision, AMEND, or Compassionate Friends, listed under "Support Organizations" in the appendix (see p. 226). You will find that women who have shared a similar experience will be good listeners and will support you.

YOUR BODY'S ADJUSTMENT

After an abortion your body will need some time to readjust. You will have some vaginal bleeding, and you may even experience some aching in your breasts. If you went through labor you may feel the general postpartum blues or other discomforts. Ask your health care provider what you might expect.

YOUR EMOTIONS/YOUR GRIEF

The abortion of a once-wanted baby because of a disability may not be a difficult event in your life or it may be heartbreaking. You may feel severely the loss of a baby you had begun to know.

Although there is a pattern of grieving, the process will be unique for every woman. Grieving is normal and necessary. Some women feel shocked and numb after an abortion, or have difficulty controlling their emotions. Some women feel fearful, anxious, depressed, or guilty. Some women say, "I have killed my baby." Other women search and yearn for reasons why their baby had a disability. They feel angry at their partner, doctor, midwife, or at God. Anger at oneself may turn into a form of depression.

The time for grieving for a once-wanted child varies among individuals. Some women have said that in the fourth to sixth month after their abortion, depression is their strongest emotion. It may repeat itself on the anniversary of the abortion. For some women seeing a disabled person evokes guilt and sadness. Some women do not want to forget that baby; others put the past behind them. Whatever your feelings are, if abortion would be your choice, remember that you are doing it out of a sense of care and concern for yourself, your fetus, and your family.

Women who have terminated their pregnancy because of a disability are only now beginning to speak about their experiences. Although parent support groups exist or are being formed around the country to help parents cope with miscarriage or stillbirth, there are still only a few groups for women to discuss their feelings about their abortion decisions based on prenatal diagnostic test results.

Sometimes the follow-up visits with your health care provider to explain the fetopsy results, or just to talk, can be beneficial. Sometimes insurance will cover this type of counseling. You may want to talk with a hospital social worker, or a bereavement specialist, to help you make sense of your feelings if you have any ambivalence about your decision.

THINKING ABOUT ANOTHER PREGNANCY

If you elect to terminate your pregnancy because of a disability, you may receive conflicting advice about having another baby. You may want to take time to recover from the pregnancy, physically and emotionally, or you may want to have another baby right away. This "in-between" time will be different for each woman. Although some professionals advise not having another child until your body readjusts and you have completed grieving or mourning the loss of this particular fetus, only you can make this decision.

Also, consider whether or not you want to know more about your baby's disability before getting pregnant again. Knowing the causes of the problem may help you decide about genetic counseling or prenatal testing before your next pregnancy.

HEALING

Everyone has an inner gift for healing. For some people healing comes from meditation. For others it is writing, teaching, painting, or other forms of spiritual development. If you have an abortion or experience a pregnancy loss, try to mobilize your intuitive spirits and allow yourself to grieve and to heal. (See the bibliography for a list of resources.)

THE CHOICE TO HAVE AN ABORTION

Why would you consider an abortion? Knowing your own reasons can make a difference in your decision-making process.

A. Check your reasons for considering an abortion.

☐ It would be the best alternative for me at this time in my life.

☐ I wouldn't want to raise a child with a disability.

☐ I could not afford (financially) to care for a disabled person.

☐ I would want to try again for a healthy baby.

☐ My partner would want me to.

☐ It would not be socially responsible to bring a disabled baby into the world.

B. Write down any other reasons.

_____

_____

_____

C. Which is the most important reason for you? Discuss this with your partner and your health care provider.

THE CHOICE NOT TO ABORT

Why are you considering NOT having an abortion? Knowing your own reasons can make a difference in your decision-making process.

A. Check your reasons for NOT wanting to have an abortion.

☐ I think I would enjoy raising a disabled baby.

☐ The disability may be minor and correctable.

☐ I would have the baby and give it up for adoption.

☐ I am grateful I even got pregnant.

☐ I just would want to let nature take its course.

B. Write down any other reasons.

_____

_____

_____

C. Which is the most important reason for you? Discuss this with your partner and your health care provider.

BOOK THREE

To Test or
Not to Test

11

Assessing Your Pregnancy "Risk"

In current obstetrical practice women are encouraged to decide about prenatal genetic testing based on the concept of risk. Before you can decide to choose prenatal testing you need to have a clear understanding of this concept and how predictions of risk are generated. If you are going to make a decision about prenatal testing based on your risk status, you need to be able to assess your own personal chances of having a baby with a disability, your "pregnancy risk."

How the term *risk* is defined depends very much on the bias of the world you live in. In many cultures, pregnancy is considered normal and healthy. Disabilities are an accepted part of society. In recent years, especially in the Western world, pregnancy has come to be perceived as a state of illness, involving risks.

This is one of the reasons that pregnant women and their fetuses are automatically assigned a category. They are either "high risk" or "low risk." How are those labels arrived at? Such factors as age, health, family history, behavior, and environment are tabulated and statistically analyzed to assess a woman's chance of having a baby with some variation.

"Low risk," obviously, means that your health and the fetus's are such that the pregnancy is likely to proceed normally. "High risk" means that you or your fetus falls into a statistical category where there is more likelihood of a condition that may affect your health or the outcome of pregnancy.

Does "low risk" mean you will absolutely have no problem and "high risk" mean you will? Of course not. These calculations are based on observations and research studies using statistical methods that compare groups of women who are considered "equal" in terms of certain genetic, environmental, or behavioral conditions. If women in a particular group have a baby with a disability more often than those who do not, then their particular characteristic is added to a list of "high-risk" factors. For example, let's consider the statement, "As a woman gets older her chance of having a baby with a chromosome problem increases." Actually, it is not her age that causes the problem. In fact, much is still unknown about the underlying causes of Down syndrome and other chromosome variations. All we can say is that, for reasons we do not understand, more babies with Down syndrome are conceived by women of thirty-eight than by women of eighteen. Suppose, to take this a step further, in twenty years we find out that Down syndrome is related to carbon monoxide. It might then turn out that a particular thirty-eight-year-old woman who breathes only pure mountain air has a much smaller chance of having a baby with Down syndrome than an eighteen-year-old who lives adjacent to a superhighway. This of course is only a hypothetical situation, but the fact is, we don't know the "whys" about many of these matters, only the figures and how they are interpreted.

Some commonly accepted risk figures are based on limited or out-of-date research study methods, undertaken when far less was known about principles of epidemiology. No two people are alike. Our bodies are unique and complex. Each person responds differently to the same factors. Therefore, most statements about our chances of having a baby with a disability are generalizations, not statements of certainty.

As we evaluate whether to choose the various prenatal tests and as we decide whether or not to be concerned with the risks of our pregnancy, we need to review the literature with care—and with a healthy skepticism.

WHAT ARE DISABILITIES?

A disability is a human variation frequently referred to as a birth defect or genetic disorder. In medical genetic terms, a birth defect is any variation of the body, either structural or chemical, that is present at birth. It is sometimes called a *congenital anomaly*. Some birth defects result from the influence of environmental factors during pregnancy. Others are spontaneous genetic changes called *new mutations*. Still others are caused by a combination of both environmental and genetic factors or by injuries during the birth process. Most commonly, birth defects are slight variations from normal and may cause only minor inconvenience. Others can cause mental or physical handicaps, and still others are incompatible with life and result in miscarriage, stillbirth, or early death.

A genetic disorder is an inherited condition that may be passed from generation to generation through the genes. It is sometimes referred to as *familial*, meaning one that runs in the family. A genetic disorder can be caused by a single gene or chromosome. Unlike birth defects, not all genetic disorders are present at birth: some appear later in life, and others may not appear in any particular child. Like birth defects, a genetic disorder has a wide range of variation, from mild to severe.

STATISTICS ON DISABILITIES

According to national data sources it has been estimated that 98 percent of babies born are healthy, and that 2 to 4 percent of all babies are born with a disability that can range from mild to severe. Theories on the causes of disabilities are speculative. About 20 percent of disabilities are thought to be caused by chance occurrences at fertilization. Other genetic conditions follow a specific pattern of inheritance and can be traced from generation to generation.

Another 20 percent of disabilities are attributed to environmental factors, when something in the environment, either inside or outside your body, affects your growing baby during pregnancy.

We really do not know the cause of the other 60 percent of all disabilities. They are thought to be influenced by a combination of genetic and environmental factors.

Many women consider prenatal tests because of the statistics like these about the occurrence of disabilities. However, though the figures are often presented as hard and true facts, the data on the number of babies born with a disability are rough. At the present time, there is no comprehensive assessment of the number, variety, and distribution of babies born with birth defects and genetic disorders. Health professionals are just beginning to document the occurrence of various disabilities as recorded on birth certificates. The reporting is sketchy. New classification systems to distinguish between minor and major disabilities are still being designed.

Before you make any decisions based on your chances of having a baby with a disability, try to find out about the reliability of the data you are basing your decision on, and carefully discuss the statistics with your health care provider.

RISK SCREENING

Many practitioners believe that by identifying risk factors early, an adverse pregnancy outcome can be prevented. If, for example, your provider believes that at age thirty you are "at risk" of having a baby with Down syndrome, s/he may offer you amniocentesis. The problem is that approaching pregnancy with a mind-set of "high risk" can serve to justify prenatal intervention that is in itself risky or inaccurate or that generates a false sense of security. For example, babies with spina bifida are most often born to women with no special risk factor. In effect, all women are possible candidates and, therefore, most women are being offered the MSAFP screening test even though the chance of having a baby with any disability at all is very slight.

Risk screening, on the other hand, can be beneficial. It can provide information to help you seek the help you need. It can help you to make decisions about pregnancy management and prenatal tests and to decide what kind of delivery you want and where you want to give birth. The next few chapters will help you begin to assess your personal profile.

If you are considered "high risk" by your provider and you agree with that assessment, you may decide to have prenatal testing and may also seek specialized care by a doctor with expertise in high-risk pregnancy. If you are considered to be at "low risk" and you agree with that assessment, you may decide not to have any of these tests. Keep in mind that even if you are in the "high-risk" category, you do not have to have any of the prenatal tests that may be offered to you. If you're "low risk," you can still decide to have one or a combination of tests.

12 | Your Genetic Profile

Gathering information about your personal and family genetic history, as well as evaluating your environment, may help you make a decision about prenatal testing.

YOUR AGE AND PREGNANCY

Many of us are delaying childbearing because of careers, advanced education, late marriages, previous infertility, or financial concerns. As a result, advanced maternal age has become a topic of widespread publicity, and the chance of a disability appearing in babies born to "older women" has become a major concern. Many women feel they are up against a biological clock because they have been told that childbearing after a certain point is unsafe.

The belief that older women are at higher risk for pregnancy complications dates back to the 1600s when "antiquated women" were said to suffer more in pregnancies than did other women. Since then, this belief has become deeply entrenched in the culture, even though no one really understands the special risks of pregnancy in older women. The conditions said to increase with maternal age include the following: difficulty with conception and fertility, early pregnancy loss or miscarriage, multiple births, placental problems, prolonged labor, and chromosome errors such as Down syndrome. Most studies have taken as an assumption that there is a maternal age effect although the causes remain unknown. And when women are considered "at risk," for this or other reasons, clinicians are often quicker to intervene in the pregnancy.

Bear in mind that most modern "older women" who consider parenthood are in much better health than women their age used to be. Their nutrition, exercise, and other health habits are probably much better than those of the women who were evaluated in previous years—and on whose records much of the current pregnancy data is based.

And even the definition of what is an "older" pregnant woman has changed. It was once considered that a woman over forty had an increased chance of having a baby with a disability. This supposedly "high-risk" age has steadily moved downward. From forty years of age, it has gone to thirty-eight, then thirty-five, and now thirty-four. In fact, some doctors feel that any woman over thirty is at "high risk" and should utilize the existing prenatal technology. Others believe that all pregnant women, regardless of age, should take advantage of their services.

Chromosome errors can occur at all ages but they increase with age because of cellular aging—our eggs get old as we do. Other possible factors may be the age of the father, or environmental exposures, such as low-frequency radiation.

Chromosome errors, which occur when the cells divide, are usually the result of too much or too little genetic material in a single sperm, in a single egg, or in the fertilized cell.

Some chromosome errors are inherited. Others occur only as an accident during the development of the fertilized egg. When a chromosome imbalance does occur, a baby may have one, none, or several disabilities that can range from mild to severe.

Some examples of chromosome errors include Down syndrome (trisomy 21), Patau syndrome (trisomy 13), Edwards syndrome (trisomy 18), Klinefelter syndrome, and Turner syndrome. Pages 211–214 contain a description of some of these conditions, the prenatal tests available to identify if a fetus is affected, and treatment options available if a baby is born with one of these conditions.

There is no magic age that separates "low risk" from "high

risk." The recommendation that all women over thirty-five have amniocentesis has statistical meaning only. A government-funded collaborative population study undertaken during the 1960s came up with age-related risk rates for having a baby with a chromosome problem like Down syndrome. The study revealed that at approximately age thirty-five, the risk of miscarriage caused by amniocentesis is less than the risk of giving birth to a baby with Down syndrome. Simply put, this is how thirty-five came to be considered the "high risk" point or the age that women were told to consider prenatal diagnosis.

Some women do not want to know their chance of having a baby with a chromosome variation. Others want to find out as much as possible. Each woman will weigh the results differently. If you are considering prenatal testing and you want to know what the popularly quoted figures are for your chances of having a baby with a chromosome problem, read the following pages.

AGE-RELATED RISKS OF CHROMOSOME ABNORMALITY

The following chart is used most often to show the probability of a chromosome variation as it relates to age. Whenever you hear or read about "risk estimates," be sure it's clear whether the risk is of having a baby with a chromosome problem at conception or at birth. Many babies conceived with a chromosome error are not actually born. An estimated 15 percent of pregnancies result in spontaneous abortion. Many of these are due to chromosome irregularities. Our bodies often recognize that the conditions are not right, and a pregnancy may be spontaneously aborted or miscarried.

As you glance at this chart, keep in mind the cautionary discussion of statistics related to obstetrical risks (see pp. 153–154).

As we have learned, risk figures can be difficult to interpret. For example, it is hard to envision the probability or chance that at age thirty the risk of Down syndrome is 1:900; is this high or low? Therefore, whenever you try to interpret your risks, try to reverse

HOW DOWN SYNDROME INCREASES
WITH MATERNAL AGE

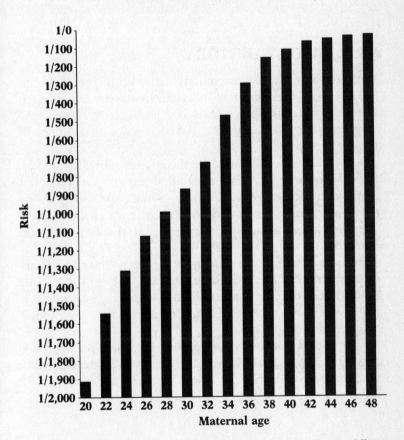

Based on data from Hook, E.B.: Rates of chromosome abnormalities at different maternal ages. *Obstet Gynecol* 1981; 58:282.

the way you think about it. For example, it may be useful to say that at thirty years of age, 1 woman out of 900 might have a baby with Down syndrome; but this also means that 899 women out of 900 women will not have a baby with Down syndrome.

Statistical assumptions that generate risk rates will not end the frustration associated with your decision-making process, but they may provide an orderly approach to begin thinking about prenatal testing.

YOUR FAMILY HISTORY

There are many genetic conditions that "run in families" and have a very specific pattern of inheritance—the pattern in which a genetic trait is distributed when it is passed from one generation to another. We can predict the occurrence of these conditions pretty definitely.

These patterns were identified in the mid 1800s by Gregor Mendel, an Austrian monk, who noticed that certain traits appeared regularly in the pea plants he bred. Some plants were short, others were long, some had flowers at the ends of their stems, others had flowers at an angle, despite the fact that he planted the same seeds.

Later researchers began to identify the genes that caused particular aberrant traits to appear in humans. These disorders are inherited and follow a particular pattern known as *Mendelian*. They are often referred to as autosomal recessive, autosomal dominant, and sex-linked.

If you suspect that you or your partner has a gene for a specific condition that runs in the family, there are well-established odds that the baby may or may not inherit that gene and/or disorder. This next section will help you to assess your family's genetic history.

AUTOSOMAL RECESSIVE INHERITANCE (HIDDEN GENES)

Each of us has what are called recessive, or hidden, genes. For example, if you have brown eyes, but your mother had blue eyes, you carry a recessive gene for blue eyes. If you marry a blue-eyed man, your child may have blue eyes, having taken one of its blue genes from the father and your blue recessive gene. You may also have a recessive gene that carries a trait for a specific disorder. You do not have to have the disorder yourself to be a carrier. It takes two parents who carry the same recessive gene to pass on the condition to a baby.

Recessive disorders are found in almost every part of the world, particularly where geography, or religious and cultural traditions encourage people to marry within their own group. This "inbreeding" makes it more likely for people to have the same genes.

If you and your baby's father have ancestors from the same area of the world, are of the same religious group, or are related to one another by blood, there may be a higher likelihood that you both carry the same gene for a recessive condition. But, of course, it's also a matter of chance that recessive genes could occur in someone from a completely different group.

Some examples of recessive conditions found more commonly in some groups than others include Tay-Sachs disease in Jewish people of Ashkenazi (Eastern European) descent; sickle-cell anemia in blacks, Hispanics, or Cape Verdeans; thalassemia in Italians, Greeks, Arabs, and Southeast Asians; and cystic fibrosis in Caucasians of Northern and Western European ancestry.

If both you and your partner are carriers of the same recessive gene for a particular disease, there is a one-in-four chance with each pregnancy of having a baby who receives a "double dose" of the genes and therefore the condition. There is a two-in-four chance of having a baby who would be unaffected with the condition but would, like you, carry the gene. There is also a one-in-four chance of having a baby who would not be affected and would not be a carrier.

The appendix contains a description of some of the more commonly known recessive conditions (see pp. 214–218).

AUTOSOMAL DOMINANT INHERITANCE

A genetic disorder may be caused by a single dominant gene. This means that it takes only one parent to pass on that gene. An individual either has the gene and has or will develop the disorder in question or does not have the gene and will never develop the condition.

If you or your partner has a dominant gene for a particular condition, the chances are one in two that your baby will be born with a gene for that condition. Of course, there's also a 50 percent chance that your baby will not have the gene and thus will not pass it on to his/her children.

Examples of genetic conditions that are inherited in a dominant fashion are achondroplasia, retinoblastoma, Huntington disease, familial hypercholesterolemia, Joseph disease, Marfan syndrome, neurofibromatosis, and tuberous sclerosis. The appendix contains a description of some of the known dominant disorders, carrier tests, available prenatal tests to identify if the fetus is affected by one of the conditions, and treatment options for a baby born with an autosomal dominant disorder (see pp. 218–220).

X-LINKED RECESSIVE (SEX-LINKED) INHERITANCE

Certain genetic disorders may be passed on by an abnormal gene on a sex chromosome. Women have two X chromosomes; men have one X and one Y chromosome. The abnormal gene is usually carried on one of the woman's X chromosomes, but only males will actually inherit the condition if they receive that chromosome.

If you carry such a gene there is a 50 percent chance that each of your sons will have the disorder, and a 50 percent chance that each son will not. There is also a 50 percent chance that each of your daughters will be a carrier. If your daughter is a carrier she has the same chances of passing the condition on to her sons as you do.

If you are not a carrier of an X-linked condition, but your baby's father has an X-linked disorder, each daughter will be a carrier of the condition, but none of your sons will be affected.

Some examples of genetic conditions inherited due to X-linked chromosomes are fragile-X syndrome, Duchenne muscular dystrophy, and hemophilia. The appendix contains a description of some X-linked conditions, available carrier tests, available prenatal tests to identify if a fetus is affected, and treatment options for a baby born with a sex-linked disorder (see pp. 220–222).

KNOWING YOUR CARRIER STATUS

A carrier is a person who has one gene for an inherited condition and one normal gene in each gene pair. A person who is a carrier carries a trait for a genetic disorder but does not have symptoms of the disorder. If you carry a gene for a certain disorder and you pass it on to your children, they may become carriers or they may inherit the disorder itself. In some instances a hidden gene expresses itself after skipping several generations.

Carrier testing can be done before or during pregnancy. It involves taking a sample of blood and analyzing it to find out whether or not you carry a gene or trait for a specific condition. The test may be performed on both parents or on other family members. To date, there are carrier tests of varying accuracy for Tay-Sachs, sickle cell, thalassemia, Duchenne muscular dystrophy, and Huntington disease. A carrier test for cystic fibrosis is in the making.

MULTIFACTORIAL INHERITANCE

Because most human variations cannot be traced to a single gene, it is often hard to determine if a disorder results from genetics, from environmental exposure, or from a combination of both. For lack of a better explanation, multifactorial disorders are thought to be due to a combination of the genes and the environment. Their pattern of transmission is not well defined.

Some examples of conditions that are inherited in this fashion are clubfoot, neural tube disorders, cleft lip/palate, congenital heart disease, diabetes mellitus, Rh disease, hypospadias, hydrocephalus, microcephalus, and pyloric stenosis. The appendix contains a description of some of these conditions, prenatal tests available to identify if a fetus is affected, and treatment options for the baby (see pp. 222–225).

HOW WAS YOUR BABY CONCEIVED?

Many women are becoming pregnant through alternative fertilization. These methods are used by women who have experienced infertility, where there is a disability that can be inherited, and among single or gay women who want to become parents. Artificial insemination, *in vitro* fertilization, and surrogacy are among the new reproductive technologies that raise special issues concerning prenatal testing. There are now a number of persons involved in reproduction: the woman who gestates and births a child (the birth mother), the woman who donates an egg without bearing the child (the genetic mother), the man who provides the sperm (the genetic father). Decisions as to who decides which person should consider prenatal testing or what tests should be applied to the fetus have become more complex as definitions of parents and arrangements change.

In the case of *in vitro* fertilization, whereby embryos may be conceived outside the womb, the "products of conception" can be screened before implantation, and those that appear "imperfect" or those that are not the right sex can be discarded. With surrogate arrangements, in which one woman carries a baby for another woman, invasive prenatal genetic tests can be mandated in the contract. Frequently, a woman who contracts with a surrogate to give birth to a child she will then raise, begins to feel anxious about fetal health in the second trimester, when genetic testing is usually performed. Surrogate contracts often contain a clause that states that if a fetus has a disability, either prenatally or at birth, the woman who was hired to carry the baby will not be paid the full amount agreed upon because she has not adequately performed her services—that of gestating the "perfect, healthy child."

In the case of artificial insemination, women now must consider whether or not they know the sperm donor. Along with requiring carrier screening tests, tests for Tay-Sachs disease, sickle-cell anemia, and thalassemia, women may want to know if the sperm has been tested once a year for antibodies to infectious diseases, such as hepatitis and AIDS. Access to the sperm donor's medical family history may also be important in order to make decisions about prenatal testing. Some women know the sperm donor; others, especially those who obtain sperm from a sperm bank, do not. There is usually strict confidentiality about whose sperm is being used in these situations, and some questions may remain unanswered.

Attention is also being given to the issue of the use of fresh or frozen sperm. In recent years, cryobanks, or frozen-semen banks, have preserved sperm in a chemical substance and stored it for many months. Proponents of cryobanking say that pregnancies that result from thawed sperm may be healthier than sperm used naturally. One theory is that frozen sperm can be periodically tested to see if it is "infected" (for example, with HIV, or AIDS). Freezing has also been said to kill off "weak and unhealthy" sperm. On the other hand, there is concern about the long-term effects on sperm quality of freezing. In general, however, offspring conceived following alternative fertilization with fresh or frozen sperm seem to be at no greater risk of being born with disabilities than are offspring conceived naturally.

Presently, there is little consensus regarding the ethical and policy issues raised by artificial insemination and screening sperm donors. Many physicians do only superficial screening of sperm donors because they feel that donors—many of whom are medical students or residents—screen themselves. One doctor recently admitted, "You are dependent on the honesty of the donor."

FOR ADOPTIVE PARENTS

If you or your partner was adopted, you may not have access to your personal or family health histories. While adoption records can be opened and, in some instances, arrangements can be made to obtain genetic histories, you may not be able to do this. In that case, you'll be relying more on feelings than on family history.

Some women decide to have the tests "just in case." On the other hand, one pregnant woman recently decided that the chances were that there probably wasn't an inherited disorder in her mother's biologic family history. She based her choices not to test on that intuitive feeling.

No matter what your family history entails or how your baby was conceived, there will always be some uncertainty about your "genetics." In making a decision about prenatal testing, you need to take into account your genetic profile, an evaluation of your environment, your belief in your body's ability to reproduce, and, perhaps most important, your feelings about disability.

13 | Your Environmental Profile

Within your womb, your baby lives in a safe and protected environment designed specifically for its growth. But alterations in that environment can occur. No one knows much about how the outside world actually affects fetal development, but some environmental elements are thought to have an influence.

Both women and men are beginning to ask questions about environmental and occupational risks to their reproductive health. Some of the questions include the following: "I am pregnant. Can the chemicals I work with harm the baby?" "I work in the operating room with anesthetic gases. Should I get a transfer while I'm pregnant?" "Should I abort this pregnancy because I have been exposed to a hazardous substance?" "Two weeks ago I had a dental X ray before I knew that I was pregnant. Will my baby be okay?" "My house needs to be sprayed with pesticides. What precautions should I take?" "I have been painting the baby's room, and now I am having headaches. Could there be any correlation?" "Three teachers in our school have had miscarriages over the past two months. There are radiowave stations nearby. Could that be the cause?"

Many health care providers are uncertain of how to approach the evaluation of environmental exposures because there is too little information available to draw conclusions. The general advice is that both men and women should minimize contact with potentially harmful substances before pregnancy. Then women should be especially careful during the first three months of pregnancy, when the fertilized cells rapidly divide to form the major body parts. If this complicated process is interfered with, certain disabilities may occur.

TERATOGENS

Environmental causes of disabilities are called *teratogens,* and the science that studies them is called *teratology.* A teratogen can be a substance, an organism, a maternal condition, or a physical agent capable of causing a disability in the fetus. Some of the commonly known and suspected teratogens are described in the following pages.

In order to call something a human teratogen, other causes must be ruled out. Then the cause-and-effect relationship must be carefully identified, defined, and proven. So far this has only been done successfully for a few agents.

It's important to remember that just because one study shows an association (for example, between caffeine and fetal disability), it doesn't mean that will always be true. Most of the research on teratogens is done on animals given large doses of the suspected substance. Therefore it is difficult to predict the effect of a small dose on human development.

It is also extremely difficult to assess a teratogen that is itself used to predict disability in the fetus. Take the example of ultrasound. When pregnant animals are exposed to high doses of ultrasound, a teratogenic effect has been demonstrated and birth defects can occur. However, because it is hard to extrapolate from an animal study and to know what a small dose might do to a human fetus, many practitioners still believe that it is safe to use ultrasound during a woman's pregnancy. The situation is still under study, and the final results are still unknown.

Since we all have a baseline risk for having a baby with a problem (there is no such thing as 0-percent risk), it's extremely hard to prove that exposure to one substance causes a particular

TERATOGENIC AGENTS IN HUMAN BEINGS

Radiation

Therapeutic
Radioiodine
Atomic weapons

Infections

Rubella virus
Cytomegalovirus
Herpes simplex virus I and
  II
Toxoplasmosis
Venezuelan equine
  encephalitis virus
Syphilis

Maternal Metabolic Imbalance

Endemic cretinism
Diabetes
Phenylketonuria
Virilizing tumors and
  metabolic conditions
Alcoholism
Hyperthermia
Rheumatic disease and
  congenital heart block

Drugs and Environmental Chemicals

Androgenic hormones
Aminopterin and
  methylaminopterin
Cyclophosphamide
Busulfan
Thalidomide
Mercury, organic
Chlorobiphenyls
Diethylstilbestrol
Diphenylhydantoin
Trimethadione and
  paramethadione
Coumarin anticoagulants
?Penicillamine
Valproic acid
Goitrogens and antithyroid
  drugs
Tetracyclines
13-cis-retinoic acid
  (Isotretinoin, Accutane)
Lithium
Methimazole and scalp
  defects

effect. Once again, it is the interaction between the genes and the environment that causes one person to have a certain outcome and another person not to. In general, exposure to potential biologic, chemical, or physical teratogens is thought to have many effects. It can cause such conditions as menstrual irregularities, decreased fertility in both males and females, an abnormality of

POSSIBLE TERATOGENS AND UNLIKELY TERATOGENS

Possible	Unlikely
?Cigarette smoking	Aspirin
?Diazepam (Valium)	Birth control pills
?Zinc deficiency	Ultrasound
?High Vitamin A	Spermicides
?Varicella	Bendectin (antinauseants)
?Binge drinking	Illicit drugs (marijuana, LSD, cocaine)
?Organic solvents (laboratory workers)	Videodisplay terminals
	Aspartame
	Anesthetics
	Rubella vaccine
	Metronidazole
	Agent Orange

the sperm, spontaneous abortion, chromosome abnormalities, low birth weight, premature births, physical disabilities, developmental delays, and childhood cancer.

In order for a teratogen to have an effect it must actually reach your embryo or fetus. In most cases—though not as far as radiation is concerned—this means that you have to have exposure to the substance through your metabolism and it must cross the placenta to the fetus. For example, a medication known to be teratogenic is thalidomide. In the 1950s, this medication was prescribed during pregnancy for morning sickness. Although at the time it was considered safe, it was later found to cause numerous disabilities.

The severity of an abnormality may increase as the amount of exposure to the teratogen increases. For example, a small dose of a teratogen may not affect your baby's development, whereas a large or a frequent dose could be lethal. The effect that a teratogen has on a growing embryo or fetus also depends on when, during its development, the embryo was exposed to the particular agent. It is thought that exposure must occur before or during the development of a specific organ in order for that organ's development to be affected.

The same teratogen does not affect every fetus in the same manner. Some researchers say that the genetic makeup of the fetus determines whether or not a teratogen will have an effect. The gene combinations that make one fetus more prone to teratogenic effects than another are not known.

THE PRENATAL ENVIRONMENT

Your Own Health

There are several medical conditions that have been linked to a higher-than-usual frequency of disabilities in the unborn baby. Usually they occur only if the condition cannot be controlled throughout a pregnancy.

If you have high blood pressure, there is a potential for toxemia of pregnancy, decreased fetal growth, increased fetal distress (less oxygen intake and heart-rate variations), and premature birth due to early labor.

The following tests may be offered: ultrasound by the eighteenth week and possibly follow-ups during the last trimester; non-stress tests (NST) during the last trimester; amniocentesis to check fetal lung maturity during the last few weeks if early labor seems likely.

If you have insulin-dependent diabetes and your blood sugar is not under control, there is a potential for having a baby with a disability (such as spina bifida); fetal distress (see above); having so large a baby there may be difficulty with delivery; or having a stillborn baby.

The following tests may be offered: maternal serum alpha-fetoprotein testing (MSAFP); frequent blood-sugar tests, including at-home blood-sugar monitoring and the hemoglobin A_{lc} blood test to measure blood-sugar control; possibly ultrasound by the eighteenth week with follow-ups during the last trimester; non-stress tests during the last trimester; possibly amniocentesis to check fetal lung maturity during the last few weeks.

If you have experienced vaginal bleeding, there is a potential for miscarriage or stillbirth, fetal distress (see above), or premature birth due to early labor.

The following tests may be offered: ultrasound to evaluate the cause and extent of bleeding; non-stress tests if bleeding occurs during the last trimester.

If you are thirty-five or older, there is a potential for chromosome variations, such as Down syndrome.

The following tests may be offered: chorionic villus sampling between nine and twelve weeks to screen for chromosome variations, such as Down syndrome; ultrasound; amniocentesis between sixteen and eighteen weeks; percutaneous umbilical blood sampling; blood-sugar tests between the twenty-eighth and thirty-second weeks because some women age thirty-five and above are considered to be at increased risk of developing temporary diabetes when pregnant.

If you are expecting twins, there is a potential for a decrease in fetal growth; an increased chance of a disability occurring; breech presentation; fetal distress; and premature labor.

The following tests may be offered: baseline ultrasound between the eighteenth and twentieth week to screen for disabilities in one or both twins; follow-ups approximately each month to check fetal growth; possibly non-stress tests and amniocentesis during the last trimester.

If you have previously had a baby with a disability, there is a potential for an increased chance of recurrence, depending on the type of disability.

The following tests may be offered: chorionic villus sampling; maternal serum alpha-fetoprotein screening; ultrasound; amniocentesis; percutaneous umbilical blood sampling.

If you have previously experienced three or more miscarriages, there is a potential for another miscarriage or premature birth.

The following tests may be offered: blood chromosome tests for father and mother before conception to screen for chromosomal variations; possibly chorionic villus sampling; ultrasound or amniocentesis to screen for disabilities in the fetus.

Prenatal testing may be offered to you if you fall into a "high risk" category. In this circumstance you may be told that your fetus requires special monitoring. Keep in mind that even if you are "at risk," the commonly discussed fetal complications do not always occur. No matter what your "risk status," you have the right to choose or refuse some of the common tests that may be offered.

If you have one of these conditions, be sure that you are being cared for by a specialized medical team that includes your obstetrical provider and a specialist for your medical condition. This team should be experienced in the care of pregnant women with the particular medical condition. These specialists may be able to guide you so that a potential problem does not occur, or they will help you to recognize it quickly if it does.

Stress
Stress is a common factor in the lives of many women, and pregnancy places an additional, unique set of pressures on them. During early pregnancy you must find a health care provider. You may wonder about the baby's health and must make a decision about prenatal testing. Then you have to decide where to give birth, what to do about your job, how to take care of the children you already have, and arrange for child care and education. Stress may be further compounded by the physical demands of pregnancy.

Some reports have suggested that maternal stress during pregnancy can contribute to premature labor and may cause a leading birth defect—low birth weight, a baby weighing less than five and a half pounds. Maternal stress can cause changes in blood pressure, heartbeat, and breathing patterns in the fetus. No one really knows what other effects chronic stress has on a developing baby.

Developing good support systems, exercising, practicing relaxation techniques, and effectively communicating what you need to your partner, employer, doctor, and family members and friends, may reduce some of the stress you feel during pregnancy.

The Food You Eat
Your diet before and during pregnancy influences fetal health. Nutritional deficiencies before and during pregnancy are said to

be the leading cause of birth disabilities all over the world. Low birth weight, metabolic toxemia of pregnancy, respiratory distress syndrome, and spina bifida are among the disorders thought to occur as a result of dietary inadequacies.

Therefore, eating a wide variety of foods—protein, dairy products, whole-grain breads and cereals, fruits and vegetables—and taking vitamin supplements are important. Eating well, however, can be difficult if you're poor, or you feel too tired to cook, or if the thought of food makes you sick, or you are just too busy during the day with work or children to sit down and eat. But now may be the time to relearn how to eat well, for your own health, as well as your baby's.

If you want to improve your diet, ask your health care provider or a nutrition specialist to help you plan menus to include an assortment of foods. Although doctors tend to be nonchalant about nutrition, and probably won't take the time to go over your dietary habits, this doesn't mean that what you eat is not important.

Almost all states have Women, Infant, and Children (WIC) programs which provide free nutrition consultation, food, and/or financial assistance to pregnant women who live on limited budgets. Get in touch with your local state-funded genetics program (listed in the appendix) for information about nutrition resources in your area. Remember, a "good diet" may help prevent certain disabilities from occurring.

Weight

Your weight gain during pregnancy is important. Doctors once told women not to gain any more than twelve pounds. Now nutrition experts are saying that a weight gain between twenty-five and thirty-five pounds is healthy during pregnancy. Of course these recommendations vary according to your individual build. Even if you are overweight before you get pregnant, you still need to gain a sufficient amount of weight to nourish your baby. Pregnancy is not a time to diet.

The following chart reveals why you need to eat well, and where the food goes in an average pregnancy.

Baby: 7.5 pounds

Uterus: 2.0 pounds

Placenta: 1.5 pounds

Amniotic fluid: 2.0 pounds

Other fluid: 4.0 pounds

Stored nutrition: 4.0 pounds

Increased mother's blood: 3.5 pounds

Increased breast tissue: 1.5 pounds

Total: 26.0 pounds

Exposure to Infections

Many women are exposed to infectious, contagious, or communicable diseases through sexual intercourse or contact with children, their colleagues at work, people on the subways, and so on. If you catch something, your fetus may also acquire an infection *in utero* or at the time of delivery. When this occurs it is referred to as a "congenital infection." Certain congenital infections known to cause fetal disabilities include German measles (rubella), chicken pox, genital herpes, toxoplasmosis (from cat feces or raw meat), hepatitis B virus, syphilis, and AIDS.

There are culture or antibody tests to check whether or not you have contracted or are immune to most infectious diseases before or during pregnancy. Some of these have become routine in pregnancy.

If you have been exposed to an infectious disease in pregnancy, there are some vaccines that can inactivate the organism without affecting the pregnancy. There are also prenatal tests (such as PUBS) that can confirm whether your baby has the infection. If you have genital herpes or chlamydia, there may be some concern about exposure to the fetus during the birth. Some health care providers routinely perform cesarean sections on women with vaginal infectious conditions. Cultures can be taken before delivery to see if an infection is active. If it is not active at the time of delivery, you should be able to deliver vaginally.

THERAPEUTIC MEDICATIONS

If possible, all drugs and chemicals should probably be avoided during pregnancy. If you do take prescription drugs, inform your health care provider that you are planning to be pregnant or that you are pregnant. Sometimes your medication can be changed or withdrawn. If you become pregnant while taking medications (even hormones like birth control pills), also notify your provider. Though only a few drugs are presently thought to cause disabilities, certain medications are thought to be more harmful than others. This includes medications that are easily obtainable and are an integral part of our culture.

Antibiotics
Antibiotics have potent effects and they should be used with caution, especially during pregnancy. Ampicillin and erythromycin are currently prescribed. Sulfa drugs and streptomycin are known teratogens and probably should be avoided. It's important to remember that sometimes the risks to the baby of not treating an infection in the mother may be greater than any effects of the drugs themselves.

Aspirin
Aspirin is a pain reliever, an anti-inflammatory, and a blood thinner. Although no relationship has been found between the use of low doses of aspirin and fetal disabilities, excessive bleeding during childbirth has been known to occur in a higher frequency in women who took aspirin during pregnancy.

Asthma Medications
Maintaining health in pregnancy by keeping asthma under the best possible control is important. Asthma medications so far have not been implicated as causes of disabilities, but when it is necessary to take these medications, it is best to do so under medical supervision and in appropriately small doses.

Anticonvulsants
The use of anticonvulsants during pregnancy is a complex issue. It is important for the developing baby that a pregnant woman's seizure disorder be kept under the best possible control, but some

seizure medications appear to carry more risk to the developing fetus than others. Dilantin, for example, has been implicated as a possible teratogen. If possible, women on anticonvulsant therapy should try to talk with a health care provider about anticonvulsant medications *before* becoming pregnant.

Valium

Several years ago, Valium was thought to be associated with cleft palate in the fetus. Recent studies have minimized the risks and indicate that small amounts of Valium probably do not significantly increase the incidence of a disability. The data remain inconclusive: withdrawal symptoms in the baby have been noted. Certainly other, nondrug, approaches to stress are preferable.

Birth Control Pills

Recent opinions conclude that a fetus is probably not at increased risk if oral contraceptives are stopped three or more months prior to conception.

If a pregnant woman continues taking the pill after conception, the risk is less clear. Congenital heart disease, structural limb changes, and other disabilities have been reported. However, the most recent studies suggest that if the developing fetus is at any increased risk from exposure to these medications, it is probably a small increase over the baseline risk and not as high as once suspected. Women are generally not encouraged to terminate pregnancy if they conceived while on the pill.

Spermicides (Jelly, Foam)

Certain studies have suggested that spermicide use at the time of conception might be harmful to the fetus. However, other experts in the area say that there is no increased risk for having a baby with a birth defect. There is no definitive answer at this time.

DRUGS

Caffeine

Recent attention has been given to the effects of caffeine on the fetus. So far most studies claim that there has not been any causal link between caffeine—whether from coffee, tea, soft drinks, or chocolate—and disabilities in the fetus. Many women continue to drink a daily cup of coffee, while others switch to a substitute drink or a naturally decaffeinated coffee. For some women caffeine can cause symptoms like irritability and increased heart rate. If you have a high intake of caffeine, you may want to talk with your health care provider or a nutritionist about cutting down.

Street Drugs, Alcohol, and Tobacco

There is little information about the effects on the developing baby of marijuana, cocaine, LSD, PCP, and mescaline. We do know that in some cases they can produce withdrawal symptoms in the newborn that continue for weeks or months after birth. They can also affect the baby's development.

Drinking or smoking during pregnancy are also thought to cause problems in the fetus. Babies born to women who smoke extensively are more likely to be low birth weight. Alcohol consumption through pregnancy can result in diminished growth and developmental problems. When and how much you drink as well as your own susceptibility all influence the consequences of alcohol during pregnancy.

Although there is no magic way to break a habit, it is possible to do so. If you take a certain drug or have certain habits, and it is hard for you to stop, ask your health care provider for referral to a specialized practitioner or center where you can get help and support. If you think you have an addiction that might affect your baby, ask for help.

RADIATION

X Rays

X rays and other medical radiation procedures deserve extra caution during pregnancy. All X rays should be avoided if possible, especially those to your lower torso, abdomen, stomach, pelvis, lower back, and kidneys, which may expose your unborn baby directly to ionizing radiation. Ionizing radiation can cause changes in the dividing cells as your fetus grows. If cellular changes occur, genetic damage can result. Since all of us vary in our radiation sensitivity, no specific amount of X ray can be considered safe.

If you must have an X ray in an emergency situation, tell your provider that you are pregnant. Whenever low-dose X rays are absolutely required (dental or other), always insist on using a lead apron as a shield over your abdomen. In such a situation, the X-ray dosage to your fetus will likely be below that believed to present a risk to fetal development.

Whenever an X ray is suggested, tell your doctor about any similar X rays you have had recently. Sometimes it is not necessary to do another one. It is also good to keep a record of the X-ray examinations you and your family have had, so you can provide this information accurately and avoid any unnecessary exposure.

Radiation in the Atmosphere

Very little is conclusively known about the sources and effects of this type of radiation. Some areas appear to have higher natural radiation than others in soil, rock, or atmosphere. In the autumn of 1987, an investigation revealed a "thin spot" in the ozone layer over the North Pole. It has been speculated that this thinning of ozone will allow more solar radiation to reach the earth, perhaps resulting in genetic changes.

Recently, radon has been found in houses and ground soil in various areas of the United States. Although the evidence is still accumulating, there is some suspicion that radon is linked to changes in gene structure or to the fetus.

LOW-FREQUENCY RADIATION (MICROWAVES)

Low-frequency radiation or electromagnetic radiation are all around us. Radio emissions and microwaves are used via radar to detect speeding cars, to transmit telephone and television signals, for government defense and security. Unfortunately, there is probably little we can do to control our exposure to these sources. Microwaves are sometimes used to treat muscle soreness, but pregnant women should avoid this unnecessary exposure.

Low-frequency radiation is also used in microwave ovens and in color televisions. No one actually knows the long-term effects on the fetus of microwave radiation exposure, just as we do not know the long-term effects of eating food irradiated by a microwave oven. High levels of microwave radiation, however, are thought to alter or kill sperm, producing temporary sterility.

The Food and Drug Administration has developed a radiation safety standard that limits the amount of microwaves that can leak from an oven throughout its lifetime, but if you use a microwave, it is advised that you stand as far away as possible (at least two feet) when it is in operation. A microwave should not be used if the door does not close firmly or if it is bent, warped, or otherwise damaged.

For more information on microwave radiation and pregnancy, get in touch with the Bureau of Radiologic Health and other agencies involved in environmental safety.

FOOD ADDITIVES

Food additives, such as nitrites, saccharin, or asparatame (Nutrasweet), that have replaced sugar in diet sodas, gelatins, whipped toppings, chewing gum, and instant drinks have been shown to be teratogenic in research animals in some studies. Again, because little is known about their effects in humans, you may want to avoid large amounts of these types of food additives.

VIDEO DISPLAY TERMINALS (VDTS)

There is limited information about the effects of video display terminal (computer screen) exposure during pregnancy. Physical complications such as eyestrain and low backaches are known to occur. Although there is no definite link to fetal disability, this is still being investigated. However, there does seem to be some research that shows an association between pregnancy loss and prolonged VDT use. If using a display terminal is part of your job, you may want to request a temporary transfer to another task and to weigh carefully the risks and the options. (See p. 182 for work-related exposure to teratogens.)

LEAD

In the early 1900s female lead workers were thought to have high rates of spontaneous abortions or babies with microcephaly (small heads). More recent research has associated relatively low levels of lead exposure with premature rupture of membranes, preterm birth, and minor disabilities. Pediatric literature documents the effect of lead on neurodevelopmental delays, claiming this effect exists from *in utero* exposure. Animal data purport that lead is a teratogen at higher doses. Exposure to lead can occur from inhaling lead-laden soil, paints, fumes, and chemicals.

EXPOSURE TO PESTICIDES

There is very little information about risk to pregnancy from pesticides, such as rat poisons or roach killers or pesticide sprays. Therefore, you may want to limit your exposure to them as much as possible before and during pregnancy. The best general advice is to avoid having your home or garden sprayed for insects or other pests during your pregnancy.

HIGH TEMPERATURES (FEVER, HOT TUBS, SAUNAS)

There is speculation that anything that raises body temperature may affect a baby's development. Prolonged fever in early pregnancy (greater than 101°F) also has been considered a possible teratogen. Living in a hot climate, however, is not a cause for concern because the body's cooling system keeps our inside temperature within normal range.

Little is known about the prolonged use of hot tubs and saunas during pregnancy, although some practitioners recommend avoiding them. Studies of women in Scandinavian countries, where bathing of this type is very common, have not shown an association with fetal disabilities.

YOUR WORKSITE

There is widespread opinion that the majority of disabilities may be related to substances in the environment that cause changes in existing genetic material. There is a host of occupational health hazards suffered by millions of workers that are not well known to the public, not reported by the press, and not well studied by researchers. Some of these hazards are encountered by women working in predominantly female jobs in environments that are not well ventilated and contain toxic fumes or chemicals.

For example, clerical workers may be exposed to substances like cleaning solvents, photocopying toners, liquid eraser products and photocopying machines that give off toxic substances. Health service workers are exposed to toxic gases and substances, infectious diseases, radiation, and chemical agents, such as sterilizing solutions. Laundry workers, food service workers, cosmetologists, and hairdressers encounter a number of hazards, such as those found in soaps, detergents, germicides, hair dyes, and microwaves. In the house we use such things as paints, oven cleaners, and sprays. Few of these substances have been evaluated for the risk they pose to pregnancy or fetal health.

Some companies have implemented policies barring women of childbearing age from certain jobs that are thought to be hazardous, on the theory that they are protecting women and any "unborn children" from the risk of miscarriage, stillbirths, and disabilities. Their primary argument is that damage from workplace exposure may occur before a woman knows she is pregnant. For example, one corporation implemented the "fetus protection policy" which excluded women aged sixteen to sixty-five from production jobs in the lead-pigment department unless they had been surgically sterilized. A number of women employees at this plant, fearful that they would be demoted from their jobs, did submit to sterilization.

Women's groups, civil rights groups, and unions contend that blanket exclusion of all women of childbearing age from certain occupations is discriminatory. They assert that eliminating or reducing the exposure of all workers—men as well as women—or transferring women who wish to become pregnant are among the more equitable solutions to the problems. In fact, there is some reason to believe that there may be gene changes in men subject to certain conditions. Such changes, of course, might affect any children they fathered.

The right to safe and healthy working conditions is assured by the Occupational Safety and Health Act of 1970. Under this act, employers must inform employees of any on-the-job hazards and must provide and maintain safe tools and equipment, an unpolluted atmosphere, and other safeguards.

In addition, many states have introduced "right to know" legislation, requiring that industries list known or suspected hazardous substances. Personnel who work with "regulated" chemicals must receive adequate training. When requested, information on chemicals in use must be provided, and chemicals must be labeled under most circumstances.

REQUESTING A JOB TRANSFER

If you are working in a situation that may pose a risk to the health of you and your unborn baby, you can request a job transfer. Some employers will follow the recommendations of a physician regarding job placement, though an employer is not required by law to transfer a pregnant worker to a safer job. If you have some strong concerns about your worksite and its potential effects on your pregnancy, speak with your employer and your health care provider. You may, however, have to face some difficult decisions about job options and birth risk.

WHOM TO CALL WITH QUESTIONS

If you are concerned about environmental exposures, get in touch with an embryologist or a pregnancy/environmental service. Teratogen registries, sometimes known as pregnancy and environmental hot lines/help lines, are being set up around the country. Most teratogen registries offer information to pregnant women, health care providers, and other persons interested in the effects of drugs, chemicals, viruses, and physical agents on maternal conditions and on the fetus. The staff usually includes a coordinator, a research teratologist, and a physician. Utilizing a variety of sources, these people collect, analyze, and disseminate information on potential teratogens. One aim of these registries is to help allay concerns you may have, or to refer pregnant women to specific services for prenatal genetic counseling (see p. 246) or testing when needed.

In some states, if you use this service, your child is offered a free pediatric examination at birth if s/he was exposed to a potential teratogen during prenatal development. Results of these examinations are usually added to a registry database and are frequently incorporated into research publications. Although most teratogen registries have up-to-date information on various substances and their effects on a developing baby, much of the information will still be vague and noncommittal because so little is actually known about the direct effects of known or suspected teratogens on human development.

If you want to get in touch with the teratogen registry that serves your area, refer to page 246 in the appendix for a listing of state genetic programs. There are also numerous feminist groups and consumer organizations that deal specifically with environmental and occupational health hazards to women. These organizations are listed in the appendix.

A WORD OF CAUTION

Concern about environmental exposure during pregnancy must be kept in proper perspective. Women have always used common sense in terms of exposure to potentially harmful substances, including prescribed drugs and other potential causes of disability. The development of a new science of teratology should not make us panic. It's unlikely that a glass of wine or a cold and fever will cause a disability. Certainly we should avoid serious contamination, but we shouldn't let fear of pollutants ruin the fun of pregnancy.

If, after reading this chapter, you consider yourself to be at "high risk" for having a baby with some sort of problem, you may decide to use one or a combination of prenatal tests. If you consider yourself to be at "low risk," you might decide not to have any of these tests. Keep in mind that even if you are in the "high risk" category, you do not necessarily have to have any of the prenatal tests that might be offered to you. If you're "low risk," you can still decide to opt for one or a combination of tests.

14 | Prenatal Self-Assessment

Now that you've learned about the concept of risk, your genetic profile, and potential environmental exposures, you're ready to put into perspective your personal decisions about prenatal testing.

Answer the questions in this prenatal health assessment, and, if necessary, consult your family and your baby's father's family for further information.

PRENATAL SELF-ASSESSMENT QUESTIONNAIRE

	YES	NO	UNCERTAIN
Do you think you have any special reason to worry about your unborn baby having a disability?			
Do you or does anyone in your family or your unborn baby's father's family have a disability or any health problem that you think "runs in the family"? These might include a birth defect, genetic disorder, or mental retardation.			

	YES	NO	UNCERTAIN
Do you have a medical condition that you think might influence fetal development, such as insulin-dependent diabetes, hypertension, or maternal PKU?			
Has this baby been conceived by artificial insemination by donor? If yes, do you have access to the donor's medical records?			
Have you or has anyone in your family had three or more miscarriages?			
Have you or has anyone in your family or your baby's father's family had stillborn children or children who died from unknown causes soon after birth?			
Are you and your baby's father blood relatives?			
Are you thirty-five years of age or older?			
Since you have been pregnant, have you taken any medications?			
Since you have been pregnant, have you smoked cigarettes?			
Since you have been pregnant, have you had alcohol, such as wine, beer?			

	YES	NO	UNCERTAIN
Since you have been pregnant, have you used any illegal drugs, such as marijuana, crack, or hallucinogens?			
Have you had any treatment with X ray or radiation during this pregnancy?			
Have you worked with chemicals, high levels of radiation, or environmental hazards during this pregnancy?			
Have you been exposed to any infectious diseases, such as German measles (rubella), toxoplasmosis, chicken pox, cytomegalovirus, or hepatitis?			
Have you been exposed to any venereal diseases, such as genital herpes, gonorrhea, chlamydia, syphilis, or AIDS?			
Have you had any treatment with anticancer drugs during this pregnancy?			
Have you or has anyone in your family or your baby's father's family ever had genetic counseling?			
Have you or has anyone in your family or your baby's father's family ever had chromosome testing?			

	YES	NO	UNCERTAIN
If you are Jewish, have you or has anyone in your family or your baby's father's family been screened for Tay-Sachs disease?			
If you are black, Hispanic, or Cape Verdean, have you or your baby's father or any close relative been screened for sickle-cell trait?			
If you are Greek or Italian, have you or your baby's father or any close relative been screened for thalassemia, Mediterranean anemia?			

If your answers are all no, your chance of having a baby with a disability is probably relatively small. You have to ask yourself whether your chance of having a side effect or complication from any test outweighs any comfort you may derive from knowing test results. Of course, as we've seen, there is, in pregnancy, no 100 percent assurance possible—either that you'll have a "perfect" baby or a baby with a problem—or even an absolutely safe and accurate test. That's life.

If your answer to one or more of the questions above is yes, you may want to talk to your health care provider or to a genetic counselor before making your decision about prenatal testing.

GENETIC COUNSELING

Genetic counseling is a relatively new service provided by specialists with advanced training in genetics. The profession was once limited to geneticists—M.D.'s or Ph.D.'s who specialized in the field of genetics. Today there is a new professional, the genetic counselor, who has a master's degree in the fields of genetics and counseling. Such people usually have backgrounds in social work, nursing, or human biology, and they are eligible for certification by the American Board of Human Genetics.

The purpose of prenatal counseling is to help you understand your chances of having a child with a disability, how disabilities occur, and the medical tests available to determine their presence or absence. You and possibly the father or other family members will meet with a counselor who will take a family history and construct a family tree (pedigree). It may be suggested that you have a physical exam or specific genetic tests. After the information has been collected, the counselor will talk with you about the chances of a disability appearing in your baby, and you and your primary health care provider will usually receive a letter summarizing the genetic counseling session.

There are a number of genetic centers around the world, primarily in large cities. They provide a coordinated approach to genetic screening, diagnosis, counseling, and follow-up, and are also often involved in research. Some genetic counseling centers, in cities as well as in rural areas, are provided in cooperation with state health departments.

Obstetricians and midwives sometimes do their own genetic counseling, although they may not have studied the subject of human genetics extensively. The field is changing so rapidly that it can be difficult for a provider in private practice to keep up with new developments. Some doctors follow the trends: if the genetics specialists currently are endorsing a given test or procedure, they flock to emulate the "leaders" and follow their recommendations. Other providers seem to take a more consistent approach. If ever you are not comfortable with the provider who is giving you genetic information or performing a test, you can ask to be referred to a specialist or you can contact your state genetic service program (p. 246) for information on the specialists in your area.

Costs for genetic counseling services vary and are generally not covered by insurance companies unless you go on to have prenatal testing or some major intervention as a result of counseling. (If you do have counseling and afterwards you decide not to have prenatal tests, ask the administrative personnel to write something like "pregnancy diagnostic evaluation" on your billing form. This phrase may help you get reimbursement.)

There are a few general points to be aware of if you are considering speaking with a genetics professional. While counselors are supposed to be nondirective and to support you in any decision that you make, many professionals have biases in favor of prenatal testing. Some prenatal tests may be recommended without enough evidence that they are safe and accurate.

Individuals are often not provided with sufficient information about disabilities. Since many counselors have not had the training or the experience of dealing with or living with disabled people, they may not always fairly portray the range of expression of the condition. Furthermore, although counseling can provide medical and statistical information, the emotional issues of prenatal testing and of disability are less fully addressed. To answer those hard questions you're probably going to need to sort out your own feelings and talk to people whose approach is less scientific.

If you do have reason to believe that you have a chance of having a baby with a disability and you choose to talk with your health care provider or to have formal genetic counseling, you may want to bring the following information with you to your meeting: (1) the Prenatal Self-Assessment Questionnaire in this chapter; (2) any other information regarding your medical history or that of your baby's father; (3) a list of all relatives who may have had a disability.

Compiling this type of information in advance may help you and your provider examine your personal profile in an organized fashion and may also help to provide a basis for your decision to choose or refuse prenatal testing.

15 | To Test or Not to Test

The time has arrived. You have had a mini-course in high-tech pregnancy, you have learned about the possible prenatal tests, their results, and your options, and you have assessed your own pregnancy risk. Now you have to decide whether to test or not to test.

THE PRENATAL GENETIC TESTING PACKAGE: A REVIEW

There are so many details that it's very hard to try to become an expert on each and every one of the prenatal tests. The following summary may be helpful at this stage.

As you separately consider each test, think about and ask your health care provider:

(1) What additional information do you need to make a decision?

(2) What are the benefits of having the test/procedure?

(3) What are the risks to you and your fetus?

(4) What are your other options/alternatives?

(5) Whose decision is it to use or refuse the test/procedure?
Yours? Your partner's? Your doctor's?

Now let's review each test.

MSAFP Screening (also see chapter 4)

Information:
Why is it considered a screening test?
How is the test performed?
What disabilities can be screened for?
What doctor and laboratory have the most experience with
this test?
What are the cut-off values? What's considered normal? Abnormal?

Benefits:
May help you decide whether further testing is indicated.
May lead to diagnosis of fetal disability if it exists.
May provide information that will be useful in later pregnancy management.

Risks:
May lead to unnecessary use of other interventions (i.e.,
ultrasound, amniocentesis); false positive and false negative interpretations; may create unnecessary anxiety.

Alternatives:
Do nothing; ultrasound; amniocentesis.

Ultrasound (also see chapter 5)

Information:
How is the procedure performed?
What type of disabilities can and cannot be identified?
What type of ultrasound machine is used?
How much experience has your doctor had in interpreting
ultrasound?

Benefits:

Determines how far along you are in your pregnancy.

Identifies number of babies you are carrying.

Can provide information about the fetal structures (brain, heart, spine, etc.).

Can possibly give an explanation for an elevated or low MSAFP test.

Can determine the position of your fetus and placenta when performing an amniocentesis or other invasive tests.

Risks:

Long-term effects are unknown; visualizing the fetus may make a decision to abort more difficult.

Alternatives:

Do nothing; MSAFP screening test; amniocentesis.

Amniocentesis (also see chapter 6)

Information:

How is the procedure performed?

What disabilities can and cannot be identified?

Who is most qualified to perform the test?

What laboratory has had the most experience analyzing the fluid and growing cell cultures?

Benefits:

Can be used to detect certain chromosome variations, metabolic disorders, and fetal sex.

May give you information on which to base decisions about labor, care after birth, adoption, or abortion.

Risks:

Failure to obtain amniotic fluid; sample mix-up; cell culture failure; maternal cell contamination; incorrect identification of your baby's sex; infection; bleeding; isoimmunization; harm to the fetus; miscarriage.

Alternatives:

Do nothing; MSAFP screening; ultrasound; CVS; PUBS.

CVS: Chorionic Villus Sampling (also see chapter 7)

Information:

How is the procedure performed?

What disabilities can and cannot be identified?

Who is most qualified to perform the test?

How many procedures have they performed?

What laboratory is best equipped to analyze the chorionic tissue?

Benefits:

Can be done in the first trimester.

Allows for early diagnosis of fetal disabilities.

Earlier results permit an earlier abortion.

Risks:

Failure to obtain chorionic tissue; chorionic tissue may not reflect genetic status of fetus; sample mix-up; cell culture failure; maternal cell contamination; incorrect identification of your baby's sex; infection; bleeding; isoimmunization; harm to the fetus; miscarriage.

Alternatives:

Do nothing; MSAFP screening; ultrasound; amniocentesis; PUBS.

PUBS: Percutaneous Umbilical Blood Sampling (also see chapter 8)

Information:

How is the procedure performed?

When is it done?

What disabilities can and cannot be identified?

Who is most qualified to perform the test?

How many procedures have they performed?

What laboratory is best equipped to analyze the fetal blood?

Benefits:

Can be used to confirm questionable findings on ultrasound in later pregnancy.

Fetal blood can be used to identify certain genetic conditions and fetal sex. It can be used to measure and/or administer substances directly to the fetus.

Risks:

Failure to obtain fetal blood; infection; perforation of the uterine arteries; bleeding; clotting in the umbilical cord; isoimmunization; harm to the fetus; premature delivery; miscarriage.

Alternatives:

Do nothing; amniocentesis.

THE EMOTIONAL PACKAGE

Many women facing prenatal tests feel ambivalent about them. The decision to have one or more tests makes women confront their feelings about their bodies and their beliefs about pregnancy, disability, abortion, and the meaning of parenthood.

For many of us the decision to test or not to test is like a roller-coaster ride with many emotional ups and downs. Some days you may think, "Yes, I want to know if there is anything wrong." Other days you feel that you do not need tests to reassure yourself that your baby is healthy. You don't want to find yourself in the midst of testing wishing you hadn't begun the process. On the other hand, you may not want to refuse the tests and then worry about the existence of rare conditions throughout your pregnancy.

Many health care providers, and perhaps your friends and family, will say you owe it to yourself and your future baby to learn all you can before it is "too late." Your own feelings may be more complex.

If most of the women you know, including your mother and your friends, have had a normal uncomplicated pregnancy, you probably expect the same for yourself. Prenatal screening may not seem important to you. On the other hand, if you have experienced a previous pregnancy that was complicated, or if other women you know have had complications or have given birth to a baby with a disability, you may fear the same thing will happen to you. These factors illustrate how personal are the decisions involved in prenatal testing.

As modern obstetrics evolves, more women are forced to decide about prenatal tests and the resulting moral and ethical questions. Just because the technology is in place, should it be used? How do you weigh the risks and benefits of the procedures when their long-term effects remain unknown? Just because something can be diagnosed, should it be? What if the test reveals that the child will possibly get Huntington disease in its thirties or forties? Or that the child may be deaf, or of small stature? Where do you draw the lines in terms of the information you want to know? And, just as you have the right to know about the sex or health of your fetus in advance of the birth, how do you maintain the right not to know?

From a political standpoint we need to ask, Who is overseeing the development of prenatal tests? Where are the consumers in the decision-making process? As prenatal tests become required, how will women's reproductive rights be affected? What will happen to women who refuse to undergo testing? Will women be held liable by insurers or courts if the baby is born with a disability? How do you make the decision to abort a fetus or continue the pregnancy if you cannot be sure how the disability will manifest itself? And what are the long-term implications of selecting who should and should not be born?

The so-called options that prenatal tests provide raise troubling questions and pose many dilemmas for pregnant women. The tests can be seen as just another way in which medicine is transforming pregnancy from something that was once a natural experience into a medicalized process that brings with it the burdens of high technology.

A TIME OF STRESS

You have only a short amount of time in which to make some of life's major decisions. Naturally the stress of this situation can affect you physically and emotionally.

Because there is an intimate, emotional connection between you and your unborn baby, the various neurohormones triggered by feelings such as calm and relaxation or fear and agitation may pass from your bloodstream across the placenta to your baby. In order to take care of yourself physically and emotionally, do relaxation exercises, eat well, and make your environment as peaceful as you can.

Try sitting in a comfortable place and focusing your awareness inside yourself. Ask yourself, "Should I have this test?" Then relax. Don't push the decision. You may also want to try a role-playing exercise, getting someone else to take the "yes" side and trying to persuade him or her not to have the tests. Then reverse roles and you be the one who is for the tests. Let the other person try to persuade you not to have them. This may clarify your thinking and your feelings.

Some women have found it helpful to keep a diary of their pregnancy and to put on paper what they're feeling about prenatal tests, disabilities, abortion, family, etc. There are other techniques for helping to clarify your thoughts and feelings. Some of these work for some people, others don't. Remember: you now know a lot about prenatal testing. You're in a very good position to make the right decision.

COUPLES CONFLICT

Conflict sometimes occurs when one person in an otherwise good relationship wants prenatal testing and the other does not. Sometimes when there is disagreement the one who does not want the tests to be performed gives in. After all, when there is opposition, it is hard to face the fact that if something later goes wrong, you didn't take advantage of the available technology. Unfortunately, some women have been given direct ultimatums: "If you don't have an amnio and this baby has Down syndrome, I am not sure I will be there for you." In this time of stress, it may be helpful for both partners to talk to other people who have faced these decisions, and also to review the relevant sections of this book together.

AMBIVALENCE

Even after you make your choice, don't be surprised if you still have lingering doubts. Most people find that they adjust to their decision as the pregnancy progresses. Spend time with people who have made similar choices and who can provide emotional support. If your partner does not support your decision, or if most of your friends have made the opposite choice, seek out new people to give you the support you need.

If your doubts about your decision intensify, it may mean that you haven't done enough homework. If so, you may need more time to evaluate the decision. You may also want to seek genetic counseling (see chapter 14) or, perhaps, you may want to seek spiritual advice.

SEEKING SPIRITUAL ADVICE

Traditionally, individuals and couples with a religious affiliation have sought the advice and counsel of their pastors and spiritual leaders. With the increasing use of genetic technology, women now face alternatives and childbearing decisions they never had to consider in the past. As a result, more and more people are seeking advice from clergy on the ethical and religious values inherent in their decisions.

In an attempt to meet the growing need for an informed clergy, interfaith conferences on genetic decision-making are being held throughout the country. Within many religious denominations there are clergy experienced in the medical, religious, and emotional complexities of decision-making. The names of some ministers, priests, and rabbis who have training in this field can sometimes be found through your state genetic program. You can also call your local clergy, hospital chaplain, or a pastoral counseling center for a referral to a qualified person of your denomination.

Most clergy will counsel within their own religious tradition. Sometimes this can place an added burden on your decision if the teaching is in conflict with your personal beliefs and needs.

TALKING ABOUT YOUR CHOICE

Many women do not talk about reproductive decisions in public. They perceive their personal and family genetic history as a private matter. Others feel that talking about their decisions helps them to gain confidence in their choices and reduces feelings of guilt. It may also leave them open to questions like, "What, you're thirty-six and you didn't have an amnio?" "Everyone has an ultrasound, why aren't you?" or, "How will you be able to live with yourself if your baby has a problem?"

If you speak openly about your decisions, be prepared for unwanted advice and perhaps criticism from people who advocate the opposite approach to pregnancy. Try to take a balanced view and to weigh the evidence, pro and con, calmly. Just as there is no assurance that whatever tests you take, you will or will not have problems, you can never be 100 percent sure you've made the right choice—about anything.

CHOOSING TO TEST

If, after reading this book, you decide to have prenatal testing, arrange to have some sort of pre-test counseling as early in your pregnancy as possible. Pre-test counseling should always be nondirective, allowing you to make your own decisions. In addition, the person who will perform the test should provide written, accurate, and complete information about the procedure, the indications for it, and its risks and benefits. Remember, even if you have decided to have prenatal testing, you can stop at any time in the testing process.

If you have prenatal testing, bring someone with you. It can be comforting to have the father or a friend close by to talk to and hold your hand, to help you relax, and to listen to your feelings after the procedure.

Many women are anxious while waiting for tests and then for the results. They worry about complications of the test or of the results themselves. Others just block the whole thing out of their mind. Be prepared for a variety of reactions.

REFUSING TO TEST

You may decide to refuse prenatal testing because you don't want to use technology to look for troubles you have no reason to expect. After all, you may reason, most people, now as always, have healthy babies. Perhaps you feel that what will be best for you and your baby is for you to live as healthfully as you can—eat nutritious food; avoid smoking, alcohol, and drugs; get fresh air and exercise; stay as clear as you can of pollution and other noxious chemicals; and do what you can to avoid unnecessary stress. If so, then that's the right way for you to go through your pregnancy. Don't let people pressure you into tests you don't want. Tell them that you would rather avoid the stress and risks of the tests than know the results, that you will learn about your baby once it's born and at that point you will deal with any unexpected situation. Remind yourself that the test results might produce unnecessary worries and risks. No amount of testing can give you the certainty that your baby will be perfectly healthy, yet chances are it will be unless you have reason to believe otherwise.

If, after reading this book, you decide not to have prenatal testing, you may feel the need for support for your decision. Talk with an empathetic friend or find another woman who made a similar choice, or become involved in a pregnancy support group to help you get through any stressful times.

DECISIONS, DECISIONS

Consider the basic risks, benefits, and alternatives related to each prenatal test as you make your decision. Complete and total reliance on health care providers has proven undependable, as witnessed by past errors in prenatal care, however well-intentioned. You may or may not trust the newer reproductive technologies even though people tell you they are safe. In that case, you may rely on the fact that the chances are very small that a baby will have a problem, unless there is reason to anticipate a particular inherited disability or disease. If there is such a health problem in one or both of your families and a test for it, learn more about it before you make your decision. This may be the time to consult the appendix (pp. 211–225) for any specific disability that concerns you.

Find a calm time and place to think about what the implications of your decision might be. Talk with your partner, your health care provider, and other women. To help you "meet" other women who have been involved in prenatal testing decisions, we have recorded their experiences here. Their voices and their experiences may help you sort out your own feelings.

Tori: "My doctor told me that MSAFP screening was just a simple, noninvasive blood test. The way it worked out was that it took two needle insertions to draw any blood. It left a big bruise on my arm, and I was a nervous wreck waiting for results. I got back an abnormal report, and I had to have it done again. The repeat test was normal, but I was really going back and forth. I didn't know which test to believe. My doctor suggested that I have an ultrasound to make sure, and then it turned out the only problem was that I was a few days further along than we thought and this accounted for the elevation on the first test. I had to spend two weeks of my pregnancy needlessly worrying about my baby's health and exposing us to unnecessary ultrasound because of that 'simple' MSAFP screening."

Lena: "I decided that the test is available, I may as well use it. The results were normal and I felt reassured that I wasn't carrying a baby with spina bifida. Now I can relax."

Marla: "My doctor was always full of fun, always kidding around. This came to an abrupt halt while he was performing the ultrasound. In a slow, heavy voice he said, 'Well, it seems as if the baby's head size is really larger than it should be at this stage.' You can imagine how I felt! I went to see a genetics specialist, and again they told me that the baby had hydrocephalus. I never thought, before I had ultrasound, about what questions might be facing me. Here I was being forced to think about whether to continue the pregnancy. I mean, I had been feeling the baby moving around inside me, and I'd seen it rolling around on the ultrasound screen, and the weeks were passing. I had to have an amniocentesis to see whether the condition was connected to some chromosome variation, and by the time I got those results I was in the twenty-third week—just inside the time for a legal abortion. I didn't know what to do. When I asked if the baby would be retarded, the doctor couldn't say. My husband and I decided to go ahead with the pregnancy, and we had to go out of state to have a shunt put into the baby's brain to drain the excess fluid. A week later I went to the genetics specialist, and it turned out that the fluid volume was reduced. When my son was born it turned out that there was a blockage and he had to have an operation and to take medicine every day. Now, he's six months old and so cute. It was tough living through, but it was worth it."

Laurie: "The first time I went to the obstetrician, I was told to be prepared for an ultrasound. When the doctor came in I asked him why he wanted me to have the test. 'To see how far along you are. I do them on all pregnant women.' I told him I didn't want to have ultrasound. It just didn't seem necessary to me and I didn't know anything about the long-term effects. After that, I decided to find somebody else, and I ended up at a midwife who didn't go around doing all these tests. I had a really good pregnancy and my baby was fine."

Sonya: "It was a real thrill for my husband and me to see the baby and watch her move on the ultrasound. The only thing is, I don't know how I would have been able to end the pregnancy if there was a problem."

Tami: "I've got spina bifida myself, and when I went to the doctor she told me I should have amniocentesis. Obviously she thought that if the fetus had my condition, I'd have an abortion. That's just like saying that my own life is worthless and that I shouldn't have been born. The only reason that I might want to know in advance if my child has spina bifida is so that I could prepare for the delivery and what the baby would need after it's born."

Marsha: "I'm thirty-seven and when I said I didn't want amnio everyone told me that I was crazy. They asked me how I could take that chance or live with myself if the baby was born with some problem. Even my doctor accused me of denying or escaping something I would rather not face. I stuck to my guns, though, and just said, 'No, leave me alone. It's my choice.' Luckily, it all turned out okay."

Sharon: "I know that a test can't guarantee me a perfect baby, but I decided to have amnio so I wouldn't have to worry all through my pregnancy. Then I did feel reassured when I found out that my baby doesn't have any of the conditions it was tested for. I had a miscarriage two years ago after I took the test, and I was afraid that that might happen again, but I knew that I would have an abortion if the baby had a disability. You can imagine how tense I felt!"

Julie: "My husband and I both carry the gene for Tay-Sachs disease and we had a baby die ten years ago. We would never have even considered having another baby without CVS [chorionic villus sampling]."

Maxine: "Well, my doctor was really pushing CVS, and I did sign the informed consent, but I didn't really have any idea of what it was going to be like. First of all, all these medical types were lined up in the room to watch what was going on. Then, when they put the suction catheter inside me and I watched on the ultrasound machine as a piece of my placenta was being torn off—it was horrible! It was one of the most barbaric procedures I could ever imagine. Then, when it was all over, they told me that the analysis was normal, but I still might want to have amnio later on to check for spina bifida, which this test didn't do. I wouldn't dream of taking any more risks or having any more tests."

Kay: "I had CVS and had a miscarriage a few days later. My doctor says that miscarriage is common early in pregnancy and that it most likely wasn't caused by the test. He thinks the miscarriage would've happened anyway, but I still wonder if CVS had anything to do with it."

Janine: "Everything was going fine. I was feeling good, eating right, and taking a prenatal exercise class. Then, during my third trimester, my doctor told me that I wasn't gaining enough weight. I had an ultrasound and then a PUBS test. It showed that my baby had an unusual chromosome condition. It was too late to have an abortion and I had to continue prenatal care with some high-risk doctors instead of with my regular obstetrician. It was the most isolating experience of my life. I wish I could have spoken to someone who had gone through the same thing before I did."

Deborah: "I could never raise a disabled child. I think it's important to be independent and happy, and I don't think that a seriously handicapped child could ever reach that goal."

Cara: "I don't want to have unnecessary testing while I'm pregnant. Why go through the pregnancy being paranoid when the chances are my baby will be fine? I hope I'm making the right choice, but if I'm not I guess I'll just have to deal with the consequences."

Madeleine: "It was great. We saw the baby and counted its fingers and toes. Our doctor saw something pointing upwards between the legs so he thinks it's a boy. It was like taking the first snapshot of our child."

Serena: "When I heard that my baby had Down syndrome, I knew I couldn't be responsible for this child twenty years from now. I've just had to make myself believe that it never happened to me."

Diana: "I've decided to have an amniocentesis. This way, if the baby does have spina bifida, I'll have a C-section. I've heard that this is easier on the baby's nervous system. I won't have an abortion, almost whatever shows."

Clea: "We went to top specialists and both of them told us that our baby only had a one percent chance of survival. Then they told us that even if it was born alive, it would have serious problems and might even die within a few days. We didn't know what to do. Take a chance? Have an abortion? It was almost a case of being too shocked to decide, so we went along with the pregnancy. Then we had a baby girl who is perfect. She doesn't have anything wrong with her at all."

Jeri: "I'm at peace with what I decided. My fetus had Down syndrome, and I knew I couldn't give her what it would take. After the abortion, I held her in my arms. I still think about her, especially around the time that I had the abortion. Sometimes I wonder if I made the right decision, but my life would have been very different otherwise. I'm really grateful that I had the option."

Lindsay: "The abortion was a painful experience. I never really imagined what it would be like alone in labor and to watch myself give birth to a twenty-two-week-old fetus. The doctors and nurses did it all the time, and they weren't very sensitive to what I was going through. I wish that I had had somebody to comfort me before, during, and after."

MAKING THE MOST OF YOUR DECISION

Any decision you make about prenatal testing is okay. Whether or not you realize it now, you have gained a new set of decision-making skills. You can share your decision-making process with other women in similar situations. Perhaps you can enlighten those practitioners with whom you are in contact. And you can apply what you have learned in this process to other decisions in your life.

The information and questions presented in this book will not end the stress that may be associated with the decision to test or not to test, but it may provide you with an approach to begin to think about what is becoming a ritual of modern pregnancy—prenatal genetic testing.

All paths involve risk. Continue to make the choices that meet your needs and those of your family. Don't rely exclusively on medical indications and recommendations. Honor your feelings, values, and your circumstances, and you will make the best decision for yourself at this time in your life.

Appendix

Description of
Disabilities

Support
Organizations

State Genetic
Service Programs

References and
Selected Readings

DESCRIPTION OF DISABILITIES

Throughout this book we have been talking about the kinds of disabilities prenatal genetic tests are searching for. To make an informed choice about the tests, you need a balanced perspective on the disabilities. The following list is not comprehensive, but it does touch upon the more common disabilities and those that some people think about during pregnancy. Bear in mind, as you go through the list, that even the "common" disabilities are relatively rare in the total number of pregnancies. Remember, also, that if you have already decided you do not have any particular reason to be concerned about having a baby with a disability, or if you have already decided not to have prenatal genetic tests in any case, you may not want to read these pages.

If you do read the individual criterion, it's important to note that some disabilities cause only minor inconvenience. Others respond to early intervention, home treatment, and medical or surgical therapies directed at relieving the symptoms. Some will require from the family an accommodation in life-style.

Only you can evaluate your own attitudes toward these conditions, your own desire to bear the child, and your own feelings about human variations.

Chromosome Variations

Earlier in the book we spoke about chromosomal variations as a cause of fetal disability (p. 157). Variations can occur in the structure or number of chromosomes, when there is too much or too little material, or when the chromosomes have pieces that are either missing or rearranged. Although chromosome variations are rare, they can occur in a woman's egg cells, a man's sperm cells, or during cell division at the time of fertilization. Chromosome variations are usually spontaneous, although there are certain types that can be inherited.

Down Syndrome

Description: This condition, also known as trisomy 21, can occur when three copies of chromosome number 21 are made, instead of two. The extra copy can appear in all or a portion of the cells. Down syndrome causes developmental disabilities, including mental retardation, which can range from mild to severe. Persons with this syndrome have a characteristic physical appearance, including short stature and flattened facial features, and may have medical complications, such as congenital heart abnormalities (see p. 224). A higher rate of hearing impairment and premature senescence have also been associated with this condition. Individuals with Down syndrome go to public school, and many can read and write.

Treatment: Early intervention, infant stimulation, and special learning programs have enabled many children with Down syndrome to exceed their predicted potential. Medical and surgical services are available to treat complications of Down syndrome. Cosmetic surgery can be performed to alter the characteristic features of a person with this condition. Life expectancy varies, depending on the severity of the condition.

Carrier tests: Carrier status for the inherited form of Down syndrome (known as a *translocation*) can be determined by family history and a blood test (chromosome analysis). If a parent does have the inherited chromosome variation, prenatal tests will be suggested.

Prenatal tests: MSAFP screening, amniocentesis, chorionic villus sampling (CVS), percutaneous umbilical blood sampling (PUBS).

Trisomy 13/Trisomy 18: There are other chromosome conditions in which an extra number 13 (Patau syndrome) or an extra number 18 (Edwards syndrome) may appear. The physical and developmental problems associated with these conditions are usually much more severe than with Down syndrome. Infants with these conditions usually do not live more than a year.

Prenatal tests: amniocentesis, chorionic villus sampling (CVS), percutaneous umbilical blood sampling (PUBS).

Sex Chromosome Variations

There may be a variation in the sex chromosome, an extra or missing X or Y. These conditions are not life-threatening.

Turner Syndrome

Description: This is a chromosomal condition that affects females. It results from an error in cell division prior to or shortly after conception.

In approximately half of the females who have this variation, only one X chromosome is present instead of the normal number of two X's. In the remaining females, the structure of one of the two X's may be altered, or mosaicism may be found. In mosaicism, some cells have the usual two X's while others have only one. This syndrome results in short stature and altered ovarian function. If the ovaries do not function, hormonal problems and infertility result. Persons with this syndrome have a characteristic physical appearance that includes short stature and neck variations. Medical problems may include altered cardiac structure and functioning. Intelligence is not affected.

Treatment: Hormonal treatments may be required; medical treatment will vary according to symptomatology.

Carrier tests: Carrier status for the inherited form of Turner syndrome (also known as *mosaicism*) can be determined by family history and a blood test (chromosome analysis). If a woman does have the inherited chromosome variation, prenatal tests will be suggested.

Klinefelter Syndrome

Description: This is a chromosomal condition affecting males. It results from an error in cell division prior to or shortly after conception. There are several chromosome variations that may occur. Generally males with this variation have an additional X chromosome (XXY instead of the usual XY). The condition may be identified during the early developmental years, but is generally recognizable before puberty. After puberty the secondary sex characteristics appear to be underdeveloped, and infertility results. Intelligence is not affected, although learning disabilities may be present.

Treatment: Hormonal treatments may be required; medical treatment will vary according to symptomatology.

Prenatal tests: amniocentesis, chorionic villus sampling (CVS), percutaneous umbilical blood sampling (PUBS).

XYY Syndrome

Description: This syndrome occurs when males have an extra Y chromosome (XYY instead of XY). It is thought to result from an error in the cell division of the sperm. The long-term effects of having this variation are only now being studied by several medical centers around the world.

Treatment: Possibly behavioral.

Prenatal tests: amniocentesis, chorionic villus sampling (CVS), percutaneous umbilical blood sampling (PUBS).

Trisomy X

Description: This is a chromosomal condition affecting females. It results from an error in cell division prior to or shortly after conception. Most females with this variation have an additional X chromosome (XXX instead of the usual XX). The presence of three X chromosomes may lead to developmental difficulties.

Prenatal tests: amniocentesis, chorionic villus sampling (CVS), percutaneous umbilical blood sampling (PUBS).

RECESSIVE CONDITIONS

Recessive conditions in the fetus can only appear when both parents carry the gene for the condition. In that case, the fetus has a one-in-four chance of inheriting the condition. This inheritance pattern, called recessive, is described in chapter 12.

Cystic Fibrosis

Description: Cystic fibrosis (CF) is a condition that occurs with a higher incidence in Caucasians with ancestry from northern or western Europe. The disability causes problems with the mucus-producing glands, so that breathing and digestion are interfered with. Symptoms include coughing, difficulty in breathing, and poor digestion. Infectious pneumonia can be a complication of the condition. Growth and sexual maturation may be delayed. Because more salt is lost in perspiration than is usual, one of the first clues to this condition is that parents notice when they kiss the baby that the skin tastes salty. Intelligence is not affected. Life expectancy is shortened.

Treatment: Persons with CF can be treated at home with physical and oxygen therapy to improve breathing. Digestion can be helped by using a combination of synthetic enzymes, salt tablets, extra vitamins, and a modified diet. Antibiotics are used to treat infections.

Carrier tests: Carrier status is currently determined by family history and possibly an experimental blood test using DNA analysis. If both parents are carriers, prenatal tests will be suggested.

Prenatal tests: amniocentesis, chorionic villus sampling (CVS), percutaneous umbilical blood sampling (PUBS).

Newborn screening: Currently one state routinely screens all newborns for this condition.

Phenylketonuria (PKU)

Description: PKU, an inborn error of metabolism, results from a missing enzyme that is necessary to process protein components. Infants with PKU appear normal at birth, but if untreated, they begin to show signs of the condition during the early years. Untreated, mental retardation of varying degrees may result. With treatment, the child can develop normally.

Treatment: A special diet low in phenylalanine can be prescribed. Restricted foods include cow's milk, regular formula, and meat. As the child grows, the blood can be tested to monitor the amount of phenylalanine. Most children are able to stop the diet at a young age.

Maternal PKU: Maternal PKU women (women who had PKU as a child), have a higher chance of having a baby with a disability. However, if a woman returns to a special diet before and during pregnancy, she can greatly reduce the chance of this occurring. A specialist in this field should be consulted before pregnancy, if possible, to establish an appropriate diet plan.

Carrier tests: Carrier status is currently determined by family history and by blood tests. If both parents are thought to be carriers, prenatal tests will be suggested.

Prenatal tests: amniocentesis, chorionic villus sampling (CVS). Percutaneous umbilical blood sampling (PUBS) can provide specimens for DNA analysis, but identifying this condition is still in the research stage.

Newborn screening: Most states routinely screen all newborns for this condition.

Rh Incompatibility

Description: Rh disease, also known as *hemolytic disease* or *erythroblastosis fetalis,* is an inherited blood disorder that results from the incompatibility of Rh blood factors in the mother and father. Those of us who have Rh factor are considered Rh-positive (Rh+); those of us without Rh factor are considered Rh-negative (Rh−). Rh disease only occurs if a baby is Rh-positive and the mother is Rh-negative.

An incompatibility can result if the fetus is Rh-positive and the blood enters a pregnant woman's bloodstream, causing it to produce antibodies that attack the fetus's blood cells. This can lead to jaundice; anemia; developmental difficulties, including mental retardation; or stillbirth. The risk of complications to the fetus in first pregnancies is not great, but it does increase with each new pregnancy.

Rh-blood incompatibility can be prevented by a vaccine which should be given to a woman with Rh blood within seventy-two hours after amniocentesis, chorionic villus sampling, percutaneous blood sampling, miscarriage, or abortion, or immediately after the birth of a baby with Rh-positive blood.

Treatment: If the fetus shows signs of the condition, blood transfusions *in utero* or immediately after birth may be performed. Labor induction may be advised to avoid prolonged effects of the antibody reaction.

Carrier tests: Blood typing before or in early pregnancy.

Prenatal tests: amniocentesis, chorionic villus sampling (CVS), percutaneous umbilical blood sampling (PUBS).

Sickle-Cell Conditions

Description: Sickle-cell disease is an inherited blood disorder. These conditions do occur with greater frequency among people of black, Hispanic, or Cape Verdean ancestry, although it is not confined to these population groups. With sickle-cell conditions, normally round blood cells take on a sickled, or crescent, shape under periods of stress, which can limit the supply of oxygen needed for the body to function. Medical problems, such as pain from joints swelling, sickle-cell crises, and early fatal infections, can occur.

Treatment: A recent study proposed treating newborns with penicillin during the first year of life to reduce some, but not all, of the childhood complications of the disorder. Treatment may involve medication for pain relief, antibiotics, and occasional blood transfusions.

Carrier tests: Carrier status can currently be determined by a blood test. If both parents are carriers, prenatal tests will be suggested.

Prenatal tests: amniocentesis, chorionic villus sampling (CVS), percutaneous umbilical blood sampling (PUBS).

Newborn screening: Some states routinely screen all newborns for this condition.

Tay-Sachs Disease

Description: Tay-Sachs disease occurs as a result of a missing enzyme necessary for breaking down complex lipid (fat) substance. The genes for this condition occur with a higher frequency among people of Eastern European (Ashkenazi) Jewish origin, but also among the Amish, Italian Catholics, and French-Canadians. Infants with Tay-Sachs disease appear to be born healthy, but at about six months, there is a deceleration of mental and physical development because of an accumulation of lipids in the nervous system. Life expectancy is three to five years.

Treatment: Medication and dietary feedings are introduced as the symptoms of the condition progress. Children with this condition may be hospitalized or may remain at home and be made comfortable.

Carrier tests: A blood test is available to determine carrier status before pregnancy, and a more specialized blood test is used during pregnancy. (Oral contraceptives, diabetes, hepatitis, and heart disease may confound the results of this test. Be sure to let your health care provider know about these variables.) If both parents are carriers, prenatal tests are indicated.

Prenatal tests: amniocentesis, chorionic villus sampling (CVS), percutaneous umbilical blood sampling (PUBS).

Thalassemia

Description: Thalassemia is a broad term for a group of inherited disorders that limit the body's ability to produce blood cells with sufficient oxygen-carrying components. Persons of Greek, Italian, Middle Eastern, Far Eastern, and Southeast Asian ancestry are thought to have a higher incidence of this condition. Children with thalassemia have an enlarged liver and spleen and may have complications of severe anemia that make them weak and tired. Life-span is generally shortened.

Treatment: Treatment frequently includes blood transfusions throughout life, beginning in the first year, and medical therapy.

Carrier tests: A blood test is currently available to determine carrier status. If both parents are carriers, prenatal tests will be suggested.

Prenatal tests: amniocentesis, chorionic villus sampling (CVS), percutaneous umbilical blood sampling (PUBS).

Newborn screening: Some states are now routinely screening all newborns for certain blood disorders, but only partial information can be obtained about the presence of thalessemia.

DOMINANT CONDITIONS

Dominant conditions in the fetus can appear when one parent carries the gene for the condition. If one parent is a carrier, the fetus has a two-in-four chance of inheriting the condition. This inheritance pattern, called *dominant,* is described in chapter 12.

Huntington Disease

Description: Huntington disease (HD), or Huntington chorea, is a late-appearing genetic disorder of the nervous system. It is thought to be caused by an imbalance of chemicals, called *neurotransmitters,* in the brain. Symptoms usually appear in adult life between the ages of thirty-five and forty-five. However, younger and older people sometimes show signs of the disorder. A characteristic hallmark of HD is uncontrollable or dancelike body movements (chorea), or spasms, frequently mistaken for nervousness or irritability. People with HD are often thought to be drunk. As HD progresses, intellectual impairment, reduction in mobility, and depression can develop.

Treatment: Psychopharmacological medications can be used to treat the symptoms of the condition.

Presymptomatic tests: The presence of the gene for HD is currently determined by family history and an experimental blood test using DNA analysis. If one parent is found to have the gene, prenatal tests will be suggested.

Prenatal tests: amniocentesis, chorionic villus sampling (CVS), percutaneous umbilical blood sampling (PUBS).

Neurofibromatosis

Description: This condition is characterized by skin and nerve growths, called *neurofibromas.* One early indication of the condition is the presence of large tan spots, known as café-au-lait spots, on the baby's skin. Complications of the condition depend on the position of the growths and what other organs are involved. For example, if the growths are near the spinal column, scoliosis can occur.

Treatment: Medical and surgical therapies directed at relieving the symptoms.

Presymptomatic tests: None.

Prenatal tests: None.

Tuberous Sclerosis

Description: This condition is generally characterized by the presence of skin lesions (such as "white spots" or hypomelanotic maculae) that vary in size, epilepsy (seizures) that begins in early life, and developmental difficulties, such as mental retardation.

Treatment: Medical and surgical therapies directed at relieving the symptoms.

Presymptomatic tests: None.

Prenatal tests: None.

X-Linked (Sex-Linked) Inheritance

X-linked conditions in the fetus are passed from females to their male children. While a woman carries the gene, it does not affect her health. Each male born to a woman who carries the gene for an X-linked condition has a one-in-two chance of inheriting the condition. Daughters will not have the condition, but may carry the gene. This inheritance pattern is described in chapter 12.

Hemophilia

Description: This bleeding condition affects males who are born without certain clotting factors, such as factor VIII, in their blood. If the blood does not clot normally, a small cut can potentially lead to serious problems. Bleeding into the joints may occur, and dental care may pose problems.

Treatment: Regular blood transfusions or injections with the clotting factor are usually required to control bleeding.

Carrier tests: Carrier status is determined by family history and by an experimental blood test using DNA analysis. If a woman is a carrier, there are prenatal tests that may indicate the sex of the unborn baby and whether he has the condition.

Prenatal tests: amniocentesis, chorionic villus sampling (CVS), percutaneous umbilical blood sampling (PUBS).

Hurler Syndrome

Description: This condition is referred to as an inborn error of metabolism of complex carbohydrates. Infants with this condition have physical abnormalities in the bones, heart, liver, and brain. During the early years of life they begin to show signs of developmental disabilities, such as mental retardation. Life expectancy is shortened.

Treatment: Medical therapies are directed at symptomatology.

Carrier tests: Carrier status can be determined by family history and by a blood test, using white blood cells.

Prenatal tests: amniocentesis, chorionic villus sampling (CVS), percutaneous umbilical blood sampling (PUBS).

Fragile-X Syndrome

Description: This condition occurs in males when a fragment of the X-chromosome has a constriction, giving it a fragile appearance. Persons with this syndrome have a characteristic physical appearance, including altered facial features and enlarged testes. This condition causes developmental difficulties, such as mental retardation and reduced fertility.

Treatment: General treatment for mental retardation usually includes early intervention, special learning and vocational programs, and medical services, prescribed as necessary.

Carrier tests: Carrier status can be currently determined by a blood test. If a woman is a carrier, prenatal tests may indicate the sex of the unborn baby and possibly whether he has the condition.

Prenatal tests: amniocentesis, chorionic villus sampling (CVS), percutaneous umbilical blood sampling (PUBS).

Duchenne Muscular Dystrophy (DMD)

Description: This condition is the most common of the childhood dystrophies. Because it is X-linked, only males are affected. The condition causes muscle weakness, progressive disability, and immobility. Muscle weakness may begin during the first few years of life and may progress, so that eventually the child needs a wheelchair. Medical complications may include serious respiratory infections. Life expectancy is short.

Treatment: Physical therapy and orthopedic devices, such as leg braces, may be required; medical and surgical treatments may be used, depending on the symptomatology.

Carrier tests: Carrier status can be currently determined by family history and possibly by experimental blood tests using DNA analysis. If a woman is a carrier, there are prenatal tests that can indicate the sex of the unborn baby and, possibly, if he has the condition.

Prenatal tests: amniocentesis, chorionic villus sampling (CVS), percutaneous umbilical blood sampling (PUBS).

Hunter Syndrome

Description: This condition affects males and is referred to as an inborn error of metabolism of complex carbohydrates (mucopolysaccharides). Infants with this condition may have medical problems affecting the heart and gradually develop developmental disabilities, such as mental retardation. Life expectancy is short.

Treatment: Medical therapies are directed at symptomatology.

Carrier tests: None.

Prenatal tests: amniocentesis, chorionic villus sampling (CVS), percutaneous umbilical blood sampling (PUBS).

MULTIFACTORIAL INHERITANCE

Multifactorial inheritance is the name given to most of the disabilities of unknown origin that are thought to be caused by the environment, or a combination of genetics and the environment. This pattern of inheritance is described in chapter 12.

Anencephaly

Description: Anencephaly, a neural tube disorder, occurs as a result of improper development of the neural tube that forms the brain. The brain and skull are malformed, usually causing a baby to be stillborn or to die shortly after birth, even with the best medical attention.

Treatment: There is no treatment.

Prenatal tests: MSAFP screening, ultrasound, amniocentesis, percutaneous umbilical blood sampling (PUBS), fetoscopy.

Spina Bifida

Description: Spina bifida, a neural tube disorder, occurs if the neural tube that forms the brain and spinal cord/column fails to develop properly. At birth the malformation may be closed over by skin or it may be open. Open spina bifida causes the formation of a sac, observable on the baby's back, that contains parts of the spinal cord. The degree of disability varies widely. It is determined by the extent of involvement of the spinal cord and the level in the back where it occurs. Spina bifida can result in a slight limp or varying degrees of paralysis, possibly with bladder and kidney problems. Intelligence is usually not affected by spina bifida *unless* there is a complication as a result of hydrocephalus (p. 224).

Treatment: Corrective surgery can be performed at birth, if necessary; orthopedic devices, such as braces or wheelchairs, and physical and medical therapies are used as needed, depending on the symptoms.

Prenatal tests: MSAFP screening, ultrasound, amniocentesis, percutaneous umbilical blood sampling (PUBS), fetoscopy.

Cleft Lip/Palate

Description: A "cleft" is a split where the upper lip and/or palate (roof of the mouth) do not grow together. These conditions may occur together or separately, and, depending on the severity, may lead to complications in breathing, speech, hearing, and eating.

Treatment: Corrective surgery at birth, dental corrections, and/or speech therapy can repair most clefts with minimal disfigurement.

Prenatal tests: Possibly ultrasound, fetoscopy.

Hydrocephalus

Description: Also known as "water on the brain," this condition occurs when the cerebrospinal fluid that cushions and protects the brain and spinal cord accumulates and cannot be reabsorbed into the bloodstream. The excess fluid can cause pressure on the brain and skull, and increase head size. It is caused by a blockage, malformation in the spinal cord, tumor, internal bleeding, or the effects of infection. With early diagnosis and treatment, physical and mental development can be expected to be normal. Untreated hydrocephalus results in developmental disabilities, such as mental retardation.

Treatment: In utero or after birth, a plastic hollow tube, called a *shunt,* is inserted into the head to drain the fluid elsewhere in the body. Surgery relieves pressure and other symptoms. However, it cannot reverse any detrimental effects that may have already occurred. Occasional complications, such as an infection or shunt malfunction, may necessitate additional surgery.

Prenatal tests: ultrasound, fetoscopy.

Clubfoot

Description: This term is used to describe a deformation or twisting of one or both feet. It is easily recognizable at birth. The condition can vary from mild to severe. It may accompany other disabilities, such as spina bifida.

Treatment: May be self-correcting after birth. Physical therapy, surgery, corrective shoes, or braces may be necessary for a limited period of time.

Prenatal tests: Possibly ultrasound, fetoscopy.

Congenital Heart Disease

Description: Structural and/or electrical variations can occur in the formation of the heart, separately or as part of a disability syndrome. The effects can range from mild to severe.

Treatment: Depending on the type of heart problem, medication may be prescribed, or heart surgery after birth may be able to correct the congenital problem.

Prenatal tests: Ultrasound, fetal echocardiography.

Cerebral Palsy (CP)

Description: Cerebral palsy is an umbrella term for a group of conditions that result from an injury to the central nervous system. *Cerebral* refers to the brain, and *palsy* describes a lack of muscle control that is often a symptom. This condition may result from malformations in the brain that occur during fetal development or because of oxygen deprivation to the brain before, during, or after birth. It can also occur if a woman has an infectious disease during pregnancy, or an Rh incompatibility; or it can occur during labor if there is insufficient oxygenation. After birth, cerebral palsy can potentially occur if there is an accidental injury to the head, lead poisoning, or neurological illness. A person may have physical symptoms that vary from poor coordination or muscle control, to muscle spasms or seizures. There may or may not be associated difficulties, such as mental retardation.

Treatment: Physical and occupational therapy may be required. Depending on symptomatology, medications or surgery may be helpful.

Prenatal tests: None. (Internal and external fetal monitoring may be done in labor to assess fetal health status.)

Mental Retardation

Description: Mental retardation, a developmental disability, is caused by a wide group of disorders of diverse origins. It originates before age five and results in significantly subaverage intelligence, a deficiency in adaptive behavior, and general delayed development. To the frequently asked question, "Is there a test that can detect this variation?" the answer must be no, though, of course, specific disorders that entail retardation can be tested for.

Treatment: Early intervention, infant stimulation, and special learning and vocational programs have enabled many individuals with mental retardation to exceed their predicted potential.

Carrier tests: None.

Prenatal tests: None.

IN THE FINAL ANALYSIS

Now that you have read this section of the appendix, remind yourself again that the occurrence of disabilities is relatively rare. Try not to let the information you've acquired make you worry. If you are considering prenatal testing, however, there is no point in avoiding thinking about the disabilities being tested for. In this, as in other life issues, knowledge is power.

SUPPORT ORGANIZATIONS

There are many voluntary organizations that provide information, educational materials, research updates, and referral and support for individual disabilities. Parents who have had experience with particular disabilities are often available to talk to you. Some of these organizations can be particularly helpful for women who are making decisions about prenatal testing. Many of these organizations can refer you to an appropriate office in your area.

This information has been adapted in part from *Reaching Out: A Directory of Voluntary Organizations in Maternal and Child Health,* published by the National Center for Education in Maternal and Child Health (1985); 8201 Greensborough Drive; Suite 600; McLean, Virginia 22102.

Abortion Support

Support For Prenatal Decision
P.O. Box 1161
San Bernardino, CA 92402
714-794-5196

Planned Parenthood Federation of America, Inc.
810 Seventh Avenue
New York, NY 10019
212-541-7800

Acoustic Neuroma (see also Deafness/Hearing Impairment and Neurofibromatosis)

Acoustic Neuroma Association
P.O. Box 398

Carlisle, PA 17013
717-249-3973

Adoption

AASK (Aid to Adoption of Special Kids)
595 Market Street, 21st Floor
San Francisco, CA 94105
415-543-AASK

Concerned United Birthparents, Inc.
184 North Main Street
Rochester, NH 03867
603-332-0122

National Adoption Center
1218 Chestnut Street
Philadelphia, PA 19107
215-925-0200

Adrenoleukodystrophy (see also Leukodystrophy)

ALD Project
c/o The JFK Institute for Handicapped Children
707 North Broadway
Baltimore, MD 21205
301-522-5409

Albinism and Hypopigmentation

NOAH (National Organization for Albinism and Hypopigmentation)
919 Walnut Street, Room 400
Philadelphia, PA 19107
215-627-3501

Arthrogryposis

Avenues (National Support Group for Arthrogryposis Multiplex
   Congenita)
P.O. Box 5192

Sonora, CA 95370
209-533-1468

Batten Disease

Children's Brain Diseases Foundation for Research
350 Parnassus, Suite 900
San Francisco, CA 94117
415-566-5402

Birth Defects/Genetics

Association of Birth Defect Children
3526 Emerywood Lane
Orlando, FL 32806
305-859-2821

Centers for Disease Control
Birth Defects Branch/Statistics
1600 Clifton Road, N.E.
Atlanta, GA 30333
404-639-3534

Federation for Children With Special Needs
312 Stuart Street
Boston, MA 02116
617-482-2915

March of Dimes Birth Defects Foundation
1275 Mamaroneck Avenue
White Plains, NY 10605
914-428-7100

National Foundation for Jewish Genetic Diseases
250 Park Avenue, Suite 1000
New York, NY 10177
212-682-5550

National Genetics Foundation, Inc.
555 West 57th Street
New York, NY 10019
212-586-5800

NORD (National Organization for Rare Disorders, Inc.)
Fairwood Professional Building
100 Route 37
New Fairfield, CT 06812
203-746-6518

Bereavement

AMEND (Aiding a Mother Experiencing Neonatal Death)
43224 Berrywick Terrace
St. Louis, MO 63128
314-487-7582

Compassionate Friends, Inc.
P.O. Box 1347
Oak Brook, IL 60521
312-323-5010

HOPING (Helping Other Parents in Normal Grieving)
Edward W. Sparrow Hospital
1215 East Michigan Avenue
Lansing, MI 48909
517-483-3606

Blindness/Visual Impairment

American Council of Blind Parents
6209 Lycoming Road
Montgomery, AL 26117
205-277-2798

American Foundation for the Blind, Inc.
15 West 16th Street
New York, NY 10011
212-620-2000
212-620-2158

The National Association for Parents of the Visually Impaired, Inc.
P.O. Box 1800806
Austin, TX 78718
512-459-6651

Breast-feeding

La Leche League International, Inc.
96616 Minneapolis Avenue
P.O. Box 1209
Franklin Park, IL 60131
312-455-7730

Nursing Mothers Counsel, Inc.
P.O. Box 50063
Palo Alto, CA 94303

Cancer

American Cancer Society, Inc.
4 West 35th Street
New York, NY 10001
212-736-3030

The Candlelighters Childhood Cancer Foundation
2025 Eye Street, N.W., Suite 1011
Washington, DC 20006
202-659-5136

Cardiovascular Disorders

American Heart Association
7320 Greenville Avenue
Dallas, TX 75231
214-750-5300

American Lung Association
1740 Broadway
New York, NY 10019
212-315-8700

Celiac-Sprue

Celiac-Sprue Association
2313 Rocklyn Drive, Suite 1
Des Moines, IA 50322
515-270-9869

Cerebral Palsy

National Easter Seal Society
2023 West Ogden Avenue
Chicago, IL 60612
312-243-8400

United Cerebral Palsy Associations, Inc.
66 East 34th Street
New York, NY 10016
212-481-6300

Childbirth

International Association of Parents and Professionals for Safe
  Alternatives in Childbirth
P.O. Box 429
Marble Hill, MO 63764
314-238-2010

International Childbirth Education Association
P.O. Box 20048
Minneapolis, MN 55420
414-542-6138

Childcare

Childcare Resource and Referral Network
809 Lincoln Way
San Francisco, CA 94122
415-661-1714

Cleft Lip/Palate (see also Craniofacial Disorders)

National Cleft Palate Association
P.O. Box 2647
Hutchinson, KS 67501
316-543-6623

Cooley's Anemia/Thalassemia

Cooley's Anemia Foundation, Inc.
105 East 22nd Street, Suite 911

New York, NY 10010
212-598-0911
800-221-3571

Cornelia de Lange Syndrome

Cornelia de Lange Syndrome Foundation, Inc.
60 Dyer Avenue
Collinsville, CT 06022
203-693-0159
800-223-8355 (outside CT)

Craniofacial Disorders (see also Cleft Lip/Palate)

National Association for the Craniofacially Handicapped
P.O. Box 11082
Chattanooga, TN 37401
615-266-1632

Cri Du Chat Syndrome

5p-Society
11609 Oakmont
Overland Park, KS 66210
913-469-8900

Cystic Fibrosis

Cystic Fibrosis Foundation
6000 Executive Boulevard
Rockville, MD 20852
301-881-9130

Deafness/Hearing Impairment

American Society for Deaf Children
814 Thayer Avenue
Silver Spring, MD 20910
301-585-5400 (Voice/TDD)

International Parents Organization
3417 Volta Place, N.W.
Washington, DC 20007
202-337-5200

Diabetes

American Diabetes Association
2 Park Avenue
New York, NY 10016
212-683-7444

Juvenile Diabetes Foundation International
60 Madison Avenue, 4th Floor
New York, NY 10010
212-889-7575

Down Syndrome

National Down Syndrome Congress
1640 West Roosevelt Road
Chicago, IL 60608
312-226-0416
800-446-3835 (outside IL)

National Down Syndrome Society
141 Fifth Avenue
New York, NY 10010
212-764-3070
800-221-4602

Dysautonomia

Dysautonomia Foundation, Inc.
370 Lexington Avenue, Room 1504
New York, NY 10017
212-889-5222

Dystonia

Dystonia Foundation
425 Hollow Road

Melville, NY 11747
516-249-7799

Ehlers Danlos Syndrome

Ehlers Danlos National Foundation
P.O. Box 1212
Southgate, MI 48195
313-282-0181

Epilepsy

Epilepsy Foundation of America
4351 Garden City Drive
Landover, MD 20785
301-459-3700

Epstein Barr Virus Syndrome

National C.E.B.V. (Chronic Epstein Barr Virus) Syndrome
  Association, Inc.
P.O. Box 230108
Portland, OR 97223
503-684-5261

Extrophy

National Support for Extrophy
5075 Medhurst Street
Solon, OH 44139
216-248-6851

Family Support

Children's Hopice International
1800 Diagonal Road, Suite 600
Alexandria, VA 22314
703-684-4464

Family Resource Coalition
230 North Michigan Avenue, Suite 1625
Chicago, IL 60601
312-726-4750

Parents Helping Parents
505 Race Street
San Jose, CA 95116
408-272-4774

Sibling Information Network
249 Glenbook Road, Box U-64
University of Connecticut
Stores, CT 06268
203-486-4034

Fragile X

The Fragile X Foundation
P.O. Box 300233
Denver, CO 80203
303-861-7508

National Fragile X Support Group
Route 8, Box 109
Bridgeton, NJ 08302
609-455-7508

Gaucher Disease

National Gaucher Foundation
1424 K Street, N.W., 4th Floor
Washington, DC 20005
202-393-2777

Glycogen Storage Disease

Association for Glycogen Storage Disease
Box 896
Durant, IA 52747
319-785-6038

Hemophilia

National Hemophilia Foundation
The Soho Building
110 Greene Street, Room 406
New York, NY 10002
212-219-8180

Huntington Disease

Hereditary Disease Foundation
606 Wilshire Boulevard, Suite 504
Santa Monica, CA 90401
213-458-4183

Huntington's Disease Foundation of America, Inc.
250 West 57th Street, Suite 2016
New York, NY 10107
212-757-0443

National Huntington's Disease Association, Inc.
1182 Broadway, Suite 402
New York, NY 10001
212-684-2781

Hydrocephalus

Hydrocephalus Parent Support Group
225 Dickinson Street, H-893
San Diego, CA 92103
619-695-3139

National Hydrocephalus Foundation
Route 1, River Road, Box 210AA
Joliet, IL 60436
815-467-6548

Immune Deficiency

Immune Deficiency Foundation
P.O. Box 586

Columbia, MD 21045
301-461-3127

Infertility

Resolve, Inc.
P.O. Box 474
Belmont, MA 02178
617-484-2424

Intraventricular Hemorrhage

I.V.H. Parents
P.O. Box 56-111
Miami, FL 33156
305-232-0381

Iron Overload

Iron Overload Diseases Association, Inc.
Harvey Building
224 Datura Street, Suite 912
West Palm Beach, FL 33401
305-659-5616

Joseph Disease

International Joseph Disease Foundation, Inc.
P.O. Box 2550
Livermore, CA 94550
415-455-0706

Kidney Disorders

National Kidney Foundation, Inc.
2 Park Avenue
New York, NY 10016
212-889-2210

Leukodystrophy (see also Adrenoleukodystrophy)

United Leukodystrophy Foundation, Inc.
2304 Highland Drive
Sycamore, IL 60178
815-895-3211

Lipid Diseases

National Lipid Diseases Foundation
1201 Corbin Street
Elizabeth, NJ 07201
201-337-2992

Liver Disorders

American Liver Foundation
998 Pompton Avenue
Cedar Grove, NJ 07009
201-857-2626
800-223-0179

Children's Liver Foundation, Inc.
155 Maplewood Avenue
Maplewood, NJ 07040
201-761-1111

Lupus (Systemic Lupus Erythematosus)

National Lupus Erythematosus Foundation, Inc.
5230 Van Nuys Boulevard, Suite 206
Van Nuys, CA 91401
818-885-8787

Malignant Hyperthermia

Malignant Hyperthermia Association of the United States
P.O. Box 3231
Darien, CT 06820
203-655-3007

Maple Syrup Urine Disease

Families with Maple Syrup Urine Disease
24806 SR 119
Goshen, IN 46526
219-862-2922

Marfan Syndrome

National Marfan Foundation
54 Irma Avenue
Port Washington, NY 11050
516-883-8712

Mental Disabilities

Association for Retarded Citizens
2501 Avenue J
Arlington, TX 76011
817-640-0204
800-433-5255

TASH: The Association for Persons With Severe Handicaps
7010 Roosevelt Way, N.E.
Seattle, WA 98115
206-523-8446

Mucopolysaccharidoses

National MPS Society, Inc.
17 Kraemer Street
Hicksville, New York 11801
516-931-6338

Multiple Sclerosis

National Multiple Sclerosis Society
205 East 42nd Street
New York, NY 10017
212-986-3240

Muscular Dystrophy

Muscular Dystrophy Association
810 Seventh Avenue
New York, NY 10019
212-586-0808

Myasthenia Gravis

Myasthenia Gravis Foundation, Inc.
15 East 26th Street, Suite 1603
New York, NY 10010
212-889-8157

Neurofibromatosis

National Neurofibromatosis Foundation, Inc.
141 Fifth Avenue, 7th Floor
New York, NY 10010
212-460-8980

Organic Acidemias

Organic Acidemia Association
1532 South 87th Street
Kansas City, KS 66111
913-422-7080

Osteogenesis Imperfecta

American Brittle Bone Society, Inc.
1256 Merrill Drive
Marshallton/West Chester, PA 19380
215-692-6248

Osteogenesis Imperfecta Foundation, Inc.
P.O. Box 838
Manchester, NH 03105
603-623-0934

Porphyria

American Porphyria Foundation
P.O. Box 11163
Montgomery, AL 36111
205-264-2564

Prader-Willi Syndrome

Prader-Willi Syndrome Association
5515 Malibu Drive
Edina, MN 55436
612-933-0113

Rehabilitation

National Organization on Disability
2100 Pennsylvania Avenue, N.W.
Washington, DC 20037
202-293-5960

National Rehabilitation Association
633 South Washington Street
Alexandria, VA 22314
703-836-1500
212-420-1500

Retinitis Pigmentosa

RP Foundation Fighting Blindness
1401 Mt. Royal Avenue
Baltimore, MD 21217
301-655-9400
301-655-1190 (TDD)

Reye Syndrome

Reye's Syndrome Society
Box RS
Benzonia, MI 49616
616-882-5521

Scleroderma

United Scleroderma Foundation, Inc.
P.O. Box 350
Watsonville, CA 95077-0350
408-728-2202

Self-Help

National Self-Help Clearinghouse
Graduate School and University Center/CUNY
33 West 42nd Street
New York, NY 10036
212-840-1259

Short Stature/Dwarfism

Little People of America, Inc.
P.O. Box 663
San Bruno, CA 94066
415-589-0695

Parents of Dwarfed Children
11524 Colt Terrace
Silver Spring, MD 20902
301-649-3275

Sickle Cell

National Association for Sickle Cell Disease, Inc.
4221 Wilshire Boulevard, Suite 360
Los Angeles, CA 90010-3503
213-936-7205
800-421-8453

Spina Bifida

Spina Bifida Association of America
343 South Dearborn Street, Room 317
Chicago IL 60604
312-663-1562

Tay-Sachs Disease

National Tay-Sachs and Allied Diseases Association
92 Washington Avenue
Cedarhurst, NY 11516
516-569-4300

Tourette Syndrome

Tourette Syndrome Association, Inc.
42–40 Bell Boulevard
Bayside, NY 11361
718-224-2999
800-237-0717

Toxoplasmosis

Toxoplasmosis Interest Group
52 Edgell Road
Gardner, MA 01440

Trisomy 18/13

Support Organization for Trisomy 18/13
478 Terrace Lane
Tooele, UT 84074
801-882-6635

Tuberous Sclerosis

American Tuberous Sclerosis Association, Inc.
P.O. Box 44
Rockland, MA 02370
617-878-5528
800-446-1211

National Tuberous Sclerosis Association, Inc.
P.O. Box 612
Winfield, IL 60190
312-668-0787

Turner Syndrome

Turner's Syndrome Society of Sacramento
2744 Tiffany West Way
Sacramento, CA 95827
916-363-3306

Twins/Multiple Births

National Organization of Mothers of Twins Clubs, Inc.
5402 Amberwood Lane
Rockville, MD 20853
301-460-6910

The Twins Foundation
P.O. Box 9487
Providence, RI 02940
401-274-6910

Williams Syndrome

Williams Syndrome Association
P.O. Box 178373
San Diego, CA 92117-0910
619-275-6628

Wilson Disease

Wilsons's Disease Association
P.O. Box 489
Dumfries, VA 22026
703-221-5532

Women's Health Organizations

A.L.A.S. (Amigas Latinas en Acción pro Salud)
c/o 47 Nichols Avenue
Watertown, MA 02172
617-924-0271

Boston Women's Health Book Collective
47 Nichols Avenue
Watertown, MA 02172
617-924-0271

The Black Women's Health Project
National Women's Health Network of Georgia
450 Auburn Avenue, Suite 157
Atlanta, GA 30312
404-659-3854

Committee for Responsible Genetics
Women and Reproductive Technology Project
186A South Street
Boston, MA 20003
617-423-0650

STATE GENETIC SERVICE PROGRAMS

Alabama

State Genetics Project
University of Alabama at
  Birmingham
University Station
Birmingham, AL 35294
(205) 934-4973

Alaska

Alaska Department of Health &
  Social Services
Division of Public Health
Health and Welfare Building
P.O. Box H-06B
Juneau, AK 99811
(907) 465-3100

Arizona

Southwest Biomedical Research
  Institute
6401 East Thomas Road
Scottsdale, AZ 85251
(602) 945-4363

Arkansas

Genetics Program
Department of Pediatrics/512 B
University of Arkansas Medical
  Sciences Campus
4301 West Markham
Little Rock, AR 72205
(501) 661-5994

California

Genetic Disease Branch
Department of Health Services
2151 Berkeley Way, Annex 4
Berkeley, CA 94704
(415) 540-2534

Colorado

Medical Affairs and Special
  Programs
Department of Health
4210 East 11th Avenue
Denver, CO 80220
(303) 331-8373

Connecticut

Maternal and Child Health
  Section
Department of Health Services
150 Washington Street
Hartford, CT 06106
(203) 566-5601

Delaware

Genetic Services and Newborn
  Screening
P.O. Box 637
Dover, DE 19903
(302) 736-4786

District of Columbia

Genetics Program
Department of Human Services
Commission of Public Health
Bureau of Maternal and Child
  Health
1875 Connecticut Avenue, N.W.
Room 804-B
Washington, DC 20009
(202) 673-6697

Florida

Children's Medical Services
Regional Genetics Program
1317 Winewood Boulevard
Tallahassee, FL 32301
(904) 488-6005

Georgia

Genetics Program
Community Health Section
Department of Human Resources
878 Peachtree Street, N.E.
Room 109
Atlanta, GA 30309
(404) 894-5122

Hawaii

Department of Health
Crippled Children's Services
    Branch
741 Sunset Avenue
Honolulu, HI 96816
(808) 734-5617

Idaho

Genetic Services Program
Idaho Department of Health &
    Welfare
Bureau of Laboratories
2220 Old Penitentiary Road
Boise, ID 83712
(208) 334-2235

Illinois

Genetic Diseases Program
Division of Family Health
Illinois Department of Public
    Health

535 West Jefferson Street
Springfield, IL 62761
(217) 785-4522

Indiana

Genetic Diseases Section
Maternal & Child Health Division
State Board of Health
1330 West Michigan Street
Box 1964
Indianapolis, IN 46206-1964
(317) 633-0805

Iowa

Birth Defects Institute, Division
    of Maternal and Child Health
Department of Health
Lucas State Office Building
Des Moines, IA 50319
(515) 281-6646

Kansas

Genetic Services
Crippled & Chronically Ill
    Children's Program
Department of Health and
    Environment
Forbes Field #740
Topeka, KS 66620
(913) 862-9360 Ext. 400

Kentucky

Genetics Program
Department for Health Service
Division of Maternal and Child
    Health
275 East Main Street
Frankfort, KY 40621
(502) 564-4430

Louisiana

Genetic Diseases Program
Office of Preventive and Public
  Health Services
Department of Health and
  Human Resources
325 Loyola Avenue, Room 613
New Orleans, LA 70112
(504) 568-5075

Maine

Genetics, Prenatal Care and
  Injury Control
Department of Human Services
Bureau of Health
Division of Maternal and Child
  Health
State House Station 11
Augusta, ME 04333
(207) 289-3311

Maryland

Division of Hereditary Disorders
Maryland Department of Health
  and Mental Hygiene
P.O. Box 13528
201 West Preston Street
Baltimore, MD 21201
(301) 225-6730

Massachusetts

Genetics Program
Massachusetts Department of
  Public Health
Division of Family Health
  Services
150 Tremont Street
Boston, MA 02111
(617) 727-5121

Michigan

Genetics Program
Michigan State Department of
  Public Health
3500 North Logan Street
P.O. Box 30035
Lansing, MI 48909
(517) 373-0657

Minnesota

Human Genetics Unit
Minnesota Department of Health
717 Delaware, S.E.
Minneapolis, MN 55446
(612) 623-5269

Mississippi

Mississippi Genetic Screening
  Program
Mississippi Department of Health
P.O. Box 1700
Jackson, MS 39215-1700
(601) 982-6571

Missouri

Missouri Genetic Disease
  Program
Missouri Department of Health
P.O. Box 570
1730 East Elm Street
Jefferson City, MO 65102
(314) 751-8157

Montana

Department of Medical Genetics
Shodair Children's Hospital
840 Helena Avenue
P.O. Box 5539

Helena, MT 59601
(406) 442-1980

Nebraska

Birth Defects Prevention
  Program
Nebraska Department of Health
301 Centennial Mall South
P.O. Box 95007
Lincoln, NE 68509
(402) 471-2647

Nevada

Bureau of Community Health
  Services
Nevada Division of Health
505 East King Street, Room 205
Carson City, NV 89710
(702) 885-4880

New Hampshire

Genetic Services Program
Bureau of Special Medical
  Services
Health and Human Services
  Building
6 Hazen Drive
Concord, NH 03301-6527
(603) 271-4533

New Jersey

Genetic Services Program
Prevention Services
Special Child Health Services
  Program
New Jersey Department of
  Health
120 South Stockton Street
CN 364

Trenton, NJ 08625
(609) 984-0775

New Mexico

Maternal and Child Health
  Bureau
New Mexico Health and
  Environment Department
P.O. Box 968
Santa Fe, NM 87504-0968
(505) 827-0020

New York

Genetics Project
Department of Health
1308 Empire State Plaza Tower
  Building
Albany, NY 12237
(518) 474-2050

North Carolina

Genetics Program
Division of Health Services
Department of Human Resources
P.O. Box 2091
Raleigh, NC 27602
(919) 733-7437

North Dakota

Medical Genetics Division
Department of Pediatrics
University of North Dakota
  Medical School
501 Columbia Road
Grand Forks, ND 58201
(701) 777-4277

Ohio

Genetics Program
Department of Health

P.O. Box 118
246 North High Street
Columbus, OH 43216
(614) 466-8804

Oklahoma

Genetics and Metabolic
  Screening
Oklahoma State Department of
  Health
1000 Northeast Tenth Street
P.O. Box 53551
Oklahoma City, OK 73152
(405) 271-4471

Oregon

Department of Medical Genetics
Oregon Health Sciences
  University
3181 S.W. Sam Jackson Park
  Road
Portland, OR 97201
(503) 225-7703

Pennsylvania

Genetic Diseases, Testing and
  Counseling Program
Division of Maternal and Child
  Health
Pennsylvania Department of
  Health
P.O. Box 90
Harrisburg, PA 17108
(717) 787-7440

Puerto Rico

Genetic Diseases Screening
  Program
University Children's Hospital

University of Puerto Rico
  Medical School
G.P.O. Box 5067
San Juan, PR 00936
(809) 765-2363

Rhode Island

Division of Family Health
Department of Health
75 Davis Street, Room 302
Providence, RI 02908
(401) 277-2312

South Carolina

South Carolina Department of
  Health and Environmental
  Control
Division of Children's Health
Bureau of Maternal and Child
  Health
2600 Bull Street
Columbia, SC 29201
(803) 758-5491

South Dakota

Birth Defects Genetics Center
University of South Dakota
  School of Medicine
414 East Clark Street
Vermillion, SD 57069
(605) 677-5623

Tennessee

Perinatal/Genetics
Maternal and Child Health
  Section
Department of Health and
  Environment
100 North Avenue North

Nashville, TN 37219
(615) 741-3335

Texas

Division of Maternal and Child
  Health
Texas Department of Health
1100 West 49th Street
Austin, TX 78756
(512) 458-7700

Utah

Department of Pediatrics
Division of Medical Genetics
University of Utah Medical
  Center
50 North Medical Drive
Salt Lake City, UT 84132
(801) 581-8943

Vermont

Vermont Regional Genetics
University of Vermont College of
  Medicine
A115 Medical Alumni Building
Burlington, VT 05405
(802) 658-4310

Virginia

Genetics Program
Bureau of Maternal and Child
  Health, Virginia Department of
  Health
109 Governor Street

Richmond, VA 23219
(804) 786-7367

Washington

Health Services Administrator
Genetics Services Section
Department of Social and Health
  Services
1704 N.E. 150th Street
Seattle, WA 98155
(206) 545-6783

West Virginia

West Virginia University Medical
  School
Morgantown, WV 26506
(304) 293-4451

Wisconsin

Statewide Genetics Services
  Network
104 Genetics Building
445 Henry Mall
University of Wisconsin
Madison, WI 53706
(608) 263-6355

Wyoming

Family Health Program
Division of Health and Medical
  Services
Hathaway Building, Fourth Floor
Cheyenne, WY 82002
(307) 777-6297

REFERENCES AND SELECTED READINGS

MSAFP Screening

Blatt, R. J. R. "To Choose or Refuse Prenatal Testing?" *GeneWatch,* Bulletin of the Committee for Responsible Genetics (1987) 3–5.

Blatt, R. J. R., and Miller, W. A., eds. *The Genetic Resource.* Special Issue on the Application of the MSAFP Screening Test. Mass. Dept. of Public Health (Autumn 1985/Winter 1986) 8–27.

DiMaio, M. S., Baumgarten, A., Greenstein, R. M., et al. "Screening for Fetal Down's Syndrome in Pregnancy by Measuring Maternal Serum Alpha-Fetoprotein Levels. *The New England Journal of Medicine* 317 (1987) 342–6.

Haddow, J. "Identifying Fetal Disorders by MSAFP Screening." *The Practitioner* 229 (August 1985) 721–725.

Knight, G. J., Palomaki, G. E., and Haddow, J. "Maternal Serum Alpha-Fetoprotein: A Problem with a Test Kit" [letter]. *The New England Journal of Medicine* 314 (20 February 1986) 516.

———. "Assessing Reliability of AFP Test Kits." *Contemporary Ob-Gyn* 30 (October 1987) 37–52.

Martin, A. O., and Liu, K. "Implications of 'Low' Maternal Serum Alpha-Fetoprotein Levels: Are Maternal Age Risk Criteria Obsolete?" *Prenatal Diagnosis* 6 (July–August 1986) 243–247.

Milunsky, A., and Alpert, E., et al. "Results and Benefits of MSAFP Screening Program." *Journal of the American Medical Association* 252 (1984) 1440–1442.

Ultrasound

Bakketeig, L. S., et al. "Randomised Controlled Trial of Ultrasonographic Screening in Pregnancy." *The Lancet* 28 (July 1984) 207–210.

Benacerraf, B., Gelman, R., and Frigoletto, F. "Sonographic Identification of Second Trimester Fetuses with Down Syndrome." *The New England Journal of Medicine* 317 (1987) 1371–1375.

Butler, Edith. "What Do We Know About Ultrasound?" *Women Wise: The New Hampshire Feminist Health Center Quarterly* 7 (Winter 1984) 9.

Patychuck, Dianne. "Ultrasound: The First Wave." *Healthsharing* 6 (Fall 1985) 25–28.

Stewart, N. "Women's Views of Ultrasonography in Obstetrics." *Birth* 13 (1986) 39–43.

"Diagnostic Ultrasound Imaging in Pregnancy." U.S. Department of Health and Human Services, National Institutes of Health, Office of Medical Applications Research, Building 1, Room 216, Bethesda, MD 20205, 1984. NIH Publication No. 84–667.

Amniocentesis

Bennett, Neil G., ed. *Sex Selection of Children.* New York: Academic Press, 1981. (See chapter 3: "Sex Selection through Amniocentesis and Selective Abortion" and chapter 5: "Decision Making and Sex Selection with Biased Technologies.")

Cohn, G. "The Amniotic Band Syndrome: A Possible Complication of Amniocentesis." *Prenatal Diagnosis* 7 (May 1987) 303–305.

Crandall, B. F., Lebherz, T. B., and Tabsh, K. "Maternal Age and Amniocentesis: Should this be lowered to 30 years?" *Prenatal Diagnosis* 6 (July–August 1986) 237–242.

Kaiser, I. H. "Amniocentesis." *Women and Health* 7 (Fall and Winter 1982) 29–38.

Neilsen, C. C. "An Encounter with Modern Medical Technology: Women's Experiences with Amniocentesis." *Women and Health* 6 (Spring and Summer 1981) 109–129.

NICHD Study Group (Dr. Daniel Seigel). "Midtrimester Amniocentesis for Prenatal Diagnosis Safety and Accuracy." *Journal of the American Medical Association* 236 (1976) 1471–1476.

Tabor, A., Madson, M., Obel, E., et al. "Randomised Controlled Trial of Genetic Amniocentesis in 4606 Low-Risk Women." *The Lancet* 7 (June 1986) 1287–1292.

Chorionic Villus Sampling

Barela, A. I., Kleinman, G. E., Golditch, I. M., et al. "Septic Shock with Renal Failure after Chorionic Villus Sampling." *American Journal of Obstetrics and Gynecology* 154 (1986) 1100–02.

Herrmann, J., and Thomas, E. "Transabdominal Chorionic Villus Sampling as an Office Procedure." *The Lancet* 1 (March 29, 1987) 747.

Lilford, R. J., Linton, L., et al. "Transabdominal Chorion Villus Biopsy: 100 Consecutive Cases." *The Lancet* 1 (June 20, 1986) 1415–1417.

Perry, T. B., et al. "Chorionic Villi Sampling: Clinical Experience, Immediate Complications, and Patient Attitudes." *American Journal of Obstetrics and Gynecology* 251 (January 1985) 161–166.

Pescia, G., and The, N., eds. *Chorionic Villus Sampling (CVS).* New York: Karger Press, 1986.

"Risk Evaluation in Chorionic Villus Sampling. Report of WHO Consultation of First Trimester Fetal Diagnosis." *Prenatal Diagnosis* 6 (Nov–Dec 1986) 451–456.

Verjaal, M., Leschot, N. J., et al. "Karyotypic Differences Between Cells from Placenta and Other Fetal Tissues." *Prenatal Diagnosis* 7 (June 1987) 343–348.

Percutaneous Umbilical Blood Sampling (PUBS)

Daffos F., et al. "Fetal Blood Sampling During Pregnancy with Use of Needle Guided by Ultrasound. 666 Consecutive Cases." *American Journal of Obstetrics and Gynecology* 153 (November 1985) 655–660.

Molecular Genetics (DNA Analysis)

Caskey, C. T. "Disease Diagnosis by Recombinant DNA Methods." *Science* 236 (1987) 1223–1229.

Chervenak, F., Isaacson, G., Mahoney, M. "Advances in the Diagnosis of Fetal Defects." *The New England Journal of Medicine* 315 (July 1986) 305–307.

Holtzman, N. "How Technology Becomes Routine Procedure. The Case of DNA-Based Tests for Genetic Disorders." *Nucleic Acid Probes in the Diagnosis of Human Genetic Disease.* New York: Alan R. Liss, 1988.

The New Human Genetics: How Splicing Life Helps Researchers Fight Inherited Disease. National Institute of General Medical Sciences, National Institutes of Health. NIH Publication No. 84, 1984.

Nichols, Eve. *Human Gene Therapy.* Cambridge, Mass.: Harvard University Press, 1988.

Genetic Risk/Counseling

Genetic Associates: Their Training, Role and Function. Irvine, Cal.: University of California, College of Medicine, Division of Clinical Genetics and Developmental Disabilities, 1981.

Holmes, L. B. "Genetic Counseling for the Older Pregnant Woman: New Data and Questions." *New England Journal of Medicine* 298 (1978) 1419–1421.

Kesler, Seymour, ed. *Genetic Counseling: Psychological Dimensions.* New York: Academic Press, 1979.

Kirz, D., Dorchester, W., Freeman, R. "Advanced Maternal Age: The Mature Gravida." *American Journal of Obstetrics and Gynecology* 152 (May 1985) 7–12.

Longo, L. "Environmental Pollution and Pregnancy: Risks and Uncertainties for the Fetus and Infant." *American Journal of Obstetrics and Gynecology* 137 (May 1980) 162–173.

Mansfield, Phyllis. *Pregnancy for Older Woman: Assessing the Medical Risks,* Westport, Conn.: Praeger, 1986.

Rapp, R. Translating the Genetic Code: The Discourse of Genetic Counseling. Unpublished manuscript.

Rimoin, D., and Emery, A., eds. *Principles and Practices of Medical Genetics.* vols. I and II. New York: Churchill Livingstone, 1983.

Shepard, T. H. *Catalog of Teratogenic Agents.* 5th ed. Baltimore: Johns Hopkins University Press, 1986.

Thompson, J., and Thompson, M. *Genetics in Medicine.* 4th ed. Philadelphia: W. B. Saunders, 1986.

Disability

Asch, A., and Fine, M. "Shared Dreams: A Left Perspective on Disability Rights and Reproductive Rights." *Radical America* 18 (July–August 1984).

Brightman, Alan, ed. *Ordinary Moments: The Disabled Experience.* Baltimore: University Park Press, 1984.

Featherstone, Helen. *A Difference in the Family.* New York: Basic Books, 1980.

Jablow, M. *Cara: Growing with a Retarded Child.* Philadelphia: Temple University Press, 1982.

Lusthaus, E., and Lusthaus, C. "The Relativity of Worth." *The Exceptional Parent* 10 (December 1980) 35–37.

Mulick, J., and Pueschel, S. M., eds. *Parent-Professional Partnerships in Developmental Disability Services.* Cambridge, Mass.: Academic Guild, 1983.

Murray, J. B., and Murray, E. *And Say What He Is: The Life of a Special Child.* Cambridge, Mass.: MIT Press, 1975.

Peuschel, S. M., Tingey, C., Rynders, J. E., Crocker, A. C., and Crutcher, D. C., eds. *New Perspectives on Down Syndrome.* Baltimore: Paul Brookes, 1987.

Rapp, R. "XYLO: A True Story." *Test-Tube Women: What Future for Motherhood?* Boston: Pandora Press, 1984.

Saxton, Marsha. "Born and Unborn: The Implications of Reproductive Technology for People with Disabilities." *Test-Tube Women: What Future for Motherhood?* Boston: Pandora Press, 1984.

Zola, Irving. "A Story Difficult to Hear and Tell." *The Exceptional Parent* 9 (June 1979) D3–D8.

Abortion

Blumberg, B. D., et al. "The Psychological Sequelae of Abortion Performed for a Genetic Indication." *American Journal of Obstetrics and Gynecology* 122 (1975) 797–808.

Fadden, R., et al. "Prenatal Screening and Pregnant Women's Attitudes Toward the Abortion of Defective Fetuses." *American Journal of Public Health* 77 (March 1987) 288–290.

Furlong, R. M., and Black, R. B. "Pregnancy Termination for Genetic Indications: The Impact on Families." *Social Work in Health Care* 10, 17–34.

Gardner, Joy. *Abortion: A Difficult Decision.* New York: Crossing Press, 1986.

Holmes-Siedle, M., Rynanen, M., et al. "Prenatal Decisions Regarding Termination of Pregnancy Following Prenatal Detection of Sex Chromosome Abnormality." *Prenatal Diagnosis* 7 (May 1987) 234–244.

Levine, K. G. "What I Thought During My Abortion." *Mademoiselle* 85 (May 1979) 113.

Petchesky, Rosalind. *Abortion and Women's Choice.* New York: Longman, 1984.

Rapp, Rayna. "The Ethics of Choice: After My Amniocentesis, Mike and I Faced the Toughest Decision of Our Lives." *Ms.* 12 (April 1984) 97.

Silver, M. "After Our Abortion, No One Said, 'I'm sorry.' " *Washington Post,* 4 June 1986.

Pregnancy Loss

Berezin, N., *After a Loss in Pregnancy.* New York: Simon & Schuster, 1982.

Borg, S., and Lasker, I., *When Pregnancy Fails: Families Coping With Miscarriage.* Boston: Beacon Press, 1981.

Freidman, R., and Gradstein, B. *Surviving Pregnancy Loss.* Boston: Little, Brown, 1982.

Johnson, J. "Stillbirth—A Personal Experience." *American Journal of Nursing* 72: 1595-1596.

Panuthos, C., and Romeo, C. *Ended Beginnings.* South Hadley, Mass.: Bergin and Garvey, 1984.

Selected Reading

Arditti, R., Klein, R. D., and Minden, S., eds. *Test-Tube Women: What Future for Motherhood?* Boston: Pandora Press, 1984.

Baskin, Yvonne. *The Gene Doctors: Medical Genetics at the Frontier.* New York: William Morrow, 1984.

Boston Women's Health Book Collective. *The New Our Bodies, Ourselves.* 3rd ed. New York: Simon & Schuster, 1985. (See chapter 17: "New Reproductive Technologies." Ruth Hubbard, with Wendy Sanford.)

Cohen, N., and Estner, L. *Silent Knife: Cesarean Prevention and Vaginal Birth after Cesarean.* South Hadley, Mass.: J. F. Bergin, 1983.

Corea, Gena. *The Mother Machine: Reproductive Technologies from Artificial Insemination to Artificial Wombs.* New York: Harper & Row, 1985.

Gallagher, Janet. "The Fetus and the Law—Whose Life Is It Anyway?" *Ms.* (September 1984) 62.

Gaskin, Ina M. *Spiritual Midwifery.* rev. ed. Summertown, Tenn.: The Book Publishing Company, 1978.

Hubbard, Ruth. "Fetal Rights and the New Eugenics." *Science for the People* 16 (March–April 1984) 7.

Hubbard, R., Henefin, M. S., and Fried, B., eds. *Biological Woman: The Convenient Myth.* Cambridge, Mass.: Schenkman, 1982.

Katz-Rothman, Barbara. *Tentative Pregnancy: Prenatal Diagnosis and the Future of Motherhood.* New York: Viking Press, 1986.

_____. *In Labor: Women and Power in the Birthplace.* New York: Norton, 1982.

Kitzinger, S. *Pregnancy and Childbirth: The Complete Book of Pregnancy and Childbirth.* rev. ed. New York: Alfred A. Knopf, 1985.

Milunsky, Aubrey. *How to Have the Healthiest Baby You Can.* New York: Simon & Schuster, 1987.

_____. *Know Your Genes.* New York: Avon Books, 1979.

Noble, E. *Childbirth With Insight.* Boston: Houghton Mifflin, 1983.

Panuthos, C. *Transformation Through Birth: A Woman's Guide.* South Hadley, Mass.: Bergin and Garvey Publishers, 1983.

Peterson, G. *Birthing Normally: A Personal Growth Approach to Childbirth.* Berkeley, Calif.: Mindbody Press, 1981.

President's Commission for the Study of Ethical Problems in Medicine and Biomedical and Behavioral Research. *Screening and Counseling for Genetic Conditions.* Washington, D.C.: U.S. Government Printing Office, 1983.

Rapp, Rayna. "The Ethics of Choice: After My Amniocentesis, Mike and I Faced the Toughest Decision of Our Lives." *Ms.* 12 (April 1984) 97.

Rush, Anne. *Getting Clear: Body Work for Women.* New York: Random House, 1973.

Grateful acknowledgment is made to the following for permission to reprint previously published material:

The Johns Hopkins University Press: two tables from *Catalog of Teratogenic Agents,* 5th edition, by Thomas H. Shepard. Reprinted by permission of The Johns Hopkins University Press, Baltimore/London, 1986, pp. xxii.

Patient Care: the article "Practical Answers on Prenatal Genetics" and the chart "How Genetic Risk Increases with Maternal Age" from the July 15, 1986, issue of *Patient Care.* Copyright © 1986 by Patient Care, Oradell, N.J. All rights reserved. Reprinted by permission of *Patient Care.*

Index

About the Author

Robin J. R. Blatt graduated from Hampshire College, trained as a registered nurse at Massachusetts General Hospital, and received her master's degree in Public Health from Boston University. She coordinates the genetics education program in Massachusetts, working with health professionals and consumers in matters relating to human genetics and prenatal testing. She lives in Cambridge with her husband and two children.

For an anthology of stories about the personal impact of genetic testing, I would appreciate hearing from women and men about factors leading to the decision to choose *or* refuse prenatal tests, and, about actual experiences with the genetic counseling and prenatal testing process. Write to:

> Committee for Responsible Genetics
> Women in Reproductive Technology Group (RJRB)
> 186A South Street
> Boston, MA 02111